50 YEARS OF DESIGN EVOLUTION

50 YEARS OF DESIGN EVOLUTION

coco raynes

images Publishing

contents

preface

The 1950s find Boston very much bare of modernism, and severely segregated by gender and ethnicity. Even in the 1960s, rather few Amelia Earharts flew the city's design skies. The then small design world (as Boston was primarily an advertising and book arts city) was controlled by men, who rarely shared devotions to modernism and were unable to accept the emerging world view of the metamorphosis in action to reach greater social and cultural responsibilities; one example, the forging of new visual languages to support the budding concepts of globalization as espoused by the Business School at Harvard—sharing equally in a global economy. Also, Boston's art institutions had barely adopted the Bauhaus manifesto, and design was still mired in an ideological battle—"fine arts" against "applied arts"—with painting and printmaking departments, focusing at best on advertising art.

In contrast, in France, President Charles de Gaulle had declared his much larger international vision of Europe, which today can be interpreted as "it is the whole of the World, that will decide its destiny," and with that he had giving his nation an internationalist and futurist direction. This was immediately reflected in the design curriculum, developed by Jean Widmer, a superb Swiss designer, for the prestigious École Nationale Supérieure des Arts Décoratifs at which Coco Raynes studied a variety of subjects in addition to classical drawings, among them graphic design, architecture and interior architecture. Before coming to the United States, she was already a fully fledged modernist designer, later influencing many of her American colleagues—rarely being influenced by them—and surprisingly, because of the freshness of her design language, very successful with her clients. She was at the cutting edge of visual exploration and committed to a philosophy of social and cultural responsibility.

Over the span of 50 years, being a world traveler, comfortable in and knowledgeable of many cultures, Ms. Raynes has held a special presence of distinction in her city on both professional and personal levels. Always reserved, exuding a sense of perfection and quiet elegance, and with a distinct and pleasant accent, on the one hand, able to converse on subjects framed by philosophers, poets and composers, and on the other, on those pragmatically posed by city planners, architects, artists, and scientists of many walks of life. With charm and sound argumentation, she has always been able to persuade with strength and determination toward higher quality, better choices, and greater appropriateness. Her design process is inclusive; instead of working just on creative hunches. She has allowed each project's spectrum to inform her as extensively as possible. From that thorough investment, she then coalesced the essences into concepts—experimenting until, finally, the distinct solutions emerged.

Even if begrudgingly, the male bastion of Boston designers had to step aside and give credit, because Ms. Raynes has strongly contributed to the maturing and expansion of responsibilities of her professional field—work for the true welfare of the public—and she is applauded and recognized—rightly so—for her ingenuity, invention, and empathy, nationally and in many countries.

—Professor Dietmar Winkler
Designer and Design Educator

Photography: Bill Miles, Boston

foreword

I have no mentor to thank. Instead, I was fortunate to have clients who gave me the opportunity to work on superb projects. Great clients inspire designers. They trust them with revolutionary concepts, encourage new ideas, and make them want to rise to the occasion. In my case, I am convinced that the intelligence of the projects made the designer.

Through my own professional evolution, I have had the pleasure of building several generations of design talent. Many of my design associates started as interns in my office and have all become independent and successful. I have tried to introduce the concept of the designer as thinker and risk-taker. There is a huge difference between following trends and innovative design—between copying and creating.

How to forgo the delicious moment when nothing can be added or deleted? To experience the unique satisfaction when the design reaches its final form? The "I have got it!" feeling. It can be the perfect spacing in typography, the utmost simplicity of a logo, or the harmony of an interior space. It is done, there is no return, and we are delighted.

However, to show progress, it is not necessary to destroy what has proven itself to be genuinely constructive and useful. Design that passes the test of time always retains a classical quality. Each era produces its own design sensibility and integrity—this holds true for all design venues from print design, to wayfinding systems, to industrial design, to architecture.

— Coco Raynes

Writing board in my first office, Cambridge, Massachusetts

1960s

I came to Boston in October of 1967, after studying in Paris at the École Nationale Supérieure des Arts Décoratifs and opened my first office in 1969. Today, this does sound very eccentric, but then, in this pre-computer era, it was feasible. All that was really necessary were two pencils, a roll of paper, the abilities to think and to draw. My first client was Muriel Cooper, Design Director of MIT Press, who entrusted me with one book cover, then three, and soon with half of the collection.

But I grew tired of being confined by the limited scale. I needed challenges, and missed the third dimension, for which I had trained and studied.

Book Covers
MIT Press
Cambridge,
Massachusetts

The restraint of these cover designs are a stark contrast with the permanent folly and eccentricities of Harvard Square in 1968. But MIT Press requested speed and the pre-computer execution dictated a certain simplicity.

Designer
Coco Raynes

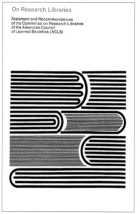

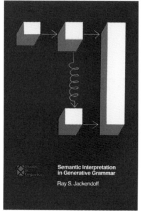
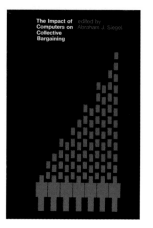

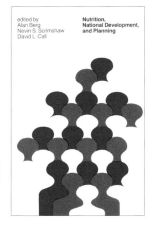

Above: This cover (signed under my maiden name) resurfaced on Twitter in 2018 with an enthusiastic comment. The completely forgotten design prompted this book. What else had vanished?

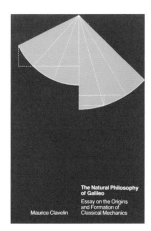

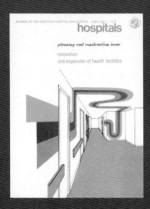

Hospitals
American Hospital Association Journal
1974 (cover), 1975, 1976

Awards of Excellence 1970, 1977
Art Directors Club of Boston

Award of Excellence 1971
American Institute of Graphic Arts

Award of Excellence for Environmental Graphics 1978
Print Magazine

1970s

The opportunity for involvement with three-dimensional environments presented itself with the invitation to work on the Neil Armstrong Air and Space Museum, in Cleveland, Ohio. It was my first exploration and application of supergraphics, a very appropriate approach to fill the museum's otherwise empty walls and a clear way of defining exhibits territorially.

This project inspired my graphic vocabulary for hospitals. Supergraphics became an effective strategy to articulate the main elements of public circulation, and their application instantaneously erased the monotonous uniformity of corridors.

Neil Armstrong
Air and Space Museum
Cleveland, Ohio

The bold graphics match the building architectural scale, and define the exhibits. The diagonal presentation evokes motion and ascent.

A circular mural around the orbit table depicts the discovery and conquest of space throughout the history of man.

Architect Arthur Klipfel
Designer Coco Raynes
Completed 1971

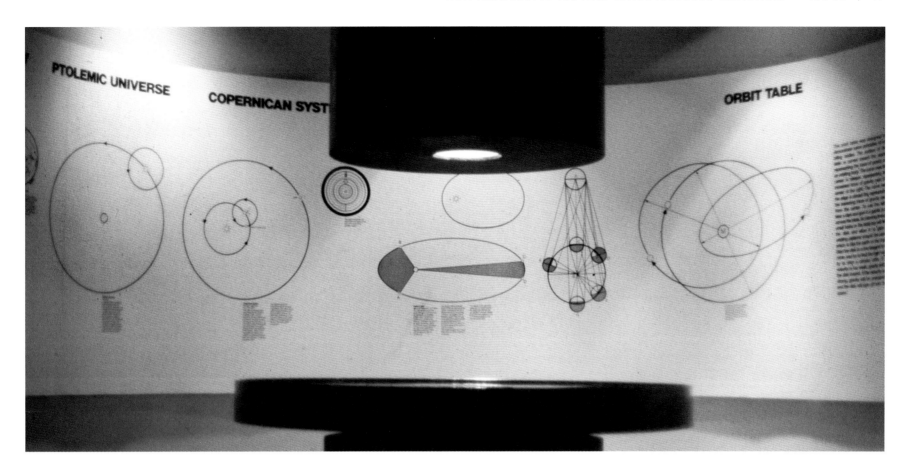

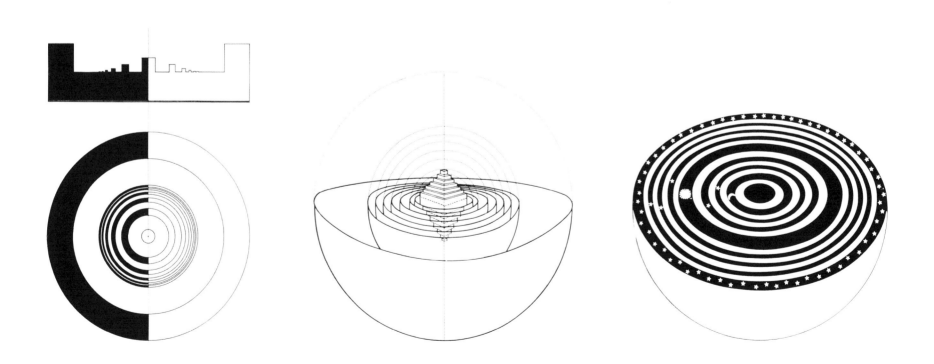

Lowell General Hospital
Lowell, Massachusetts
Supergraphics

The corridors, which all looked alike, were disorienting. Giant stripes, easy and economical to paint, brought life to the bare walls.

Designer
Coco Raynes

Completed
1973

Right: One day before the presentation, and all of a sudden I was not so sure about the scale. I went home and tested the design on my own living room wall.

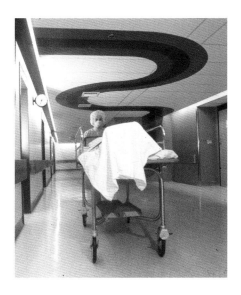

In an attempt to alleviate the patient's anxiety, the surprising stripes along the corridor accompanied them to surgery.

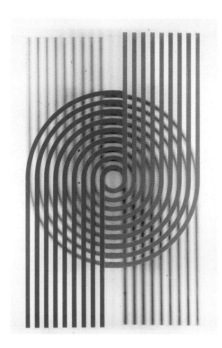 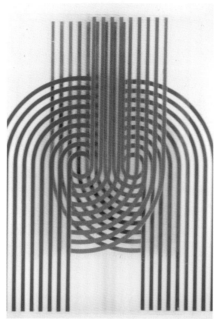 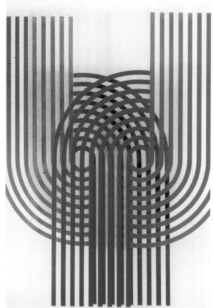 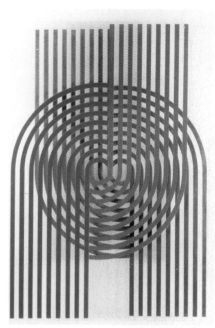

Museum of Modern Art
New York City
Graphics in Motion

Two hanging acrylic panels, set in motion by the slightest air movement, create unlimited optical effects.

They were sold at the MoMA gift store in New York City.

Designer
Coco Raynes

Completed
1970

Coolidge Hall, Harvard University
Cambridge, Massachusetts
Graphics in Motion

The scale has changed, but the same playful idea was applied to the glass partition, which provided seclusion for a lobby area for private gatherings.

Designer
Coco Raynes

Completed
1976

New England Deaconess Hospital
Boston, Massachusetts
Supergraphics

The old hospital complex comprised eleven buildings built in the early twentieth century. To explain the circulation at a glance—meaning to go right or left—an orientation diagram translated the maze of corridors and the buildings' sequential order, subway style.

The stairs and elevator doors were boldly marked to add order and visibility.

The underground corridor system, which linked the Deaconess to the Joslin Diabetes Center and Joslin Clinic, was a very disconcerting place where one could easily feel uncomfortable. The giant building names added a sense of security and led staff and visitors to their desired destination.

Designer
Coco Raynes

Completed
1974

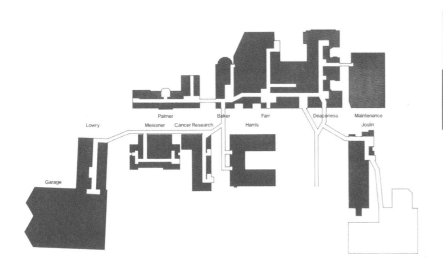

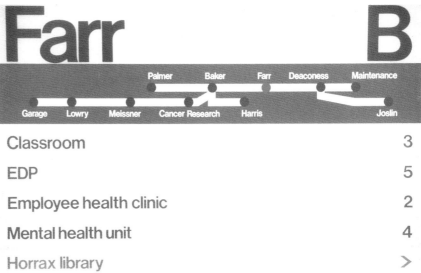

Farr   B

| | | Palmer | Baker | Farr | Deaconess | Maintenance |
| Garage | Lowry | Meissner | Cancer Research | Harris | | Joslin |

Classroom	3
EDP	5
Employee health clinic	2
Mental health unit	4
Horrax library	>

Massachusetts Eye and Ear Infirmary
Boston, Massachusetts
Supergraphics

The idea of stamping the elevator and stair doors with giant labels was repeated. In this context, it permitted patients with very little vision to perceive the elements of vertical circulation from a distance.

In an operating room, a pattern of very vivid colors helped the patient undergoing eye surgery—and who was not asleep—to focus as directed by the surgeon.

Given the insufficient number of elevators, the staff was encouraged to use stairs. Each stair landing received a giant numeral—a colorful promenade.

Designer Coco Raynes
Completed 1974

On the pediatric floor, I invited the young patients to design their own door sign, which they could change as often as they pleased; a small attempt toward relieving anxiety.

The corridors became a permanent drawing exhibit, with the drawings positioned below the serious information.

To diminish the amount of required signs, the comprehensive grid was designed to allow text, symbols, and inserts within a single frame.

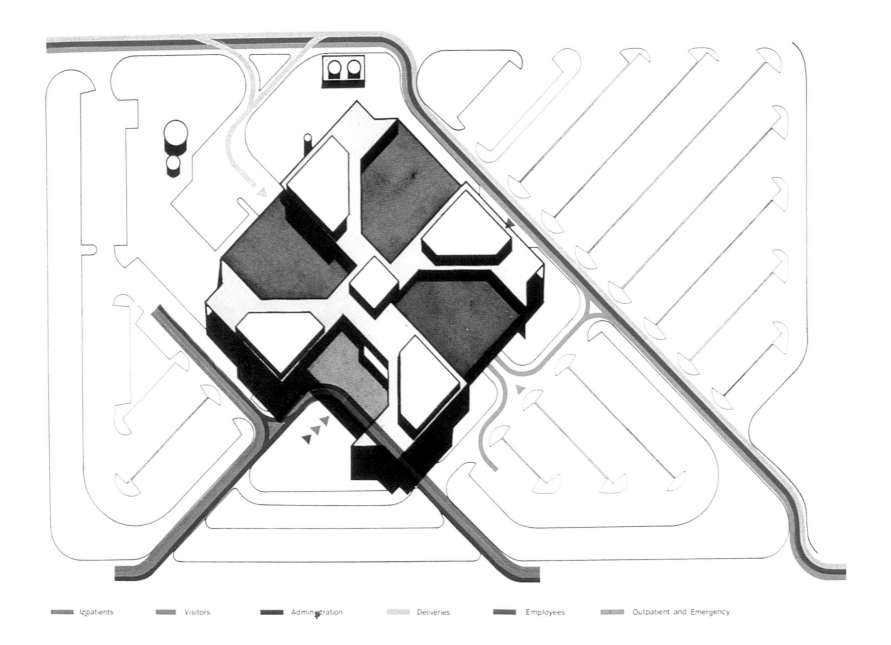

Inpatients   Visitors   Administration   Deliveries   Employees   Outpatient and Emergency

Staten Island University Hospital New York

Separate entrances where planned for the public and staff.

The color-coded system delineated the entrances and was used consistently on the pylons, directory listings, and floor diagrams.

Nursing Unit 4A	→
	→
	←
	→
	→
Admitting & Discharge	1
Business Office	1
Cafeteria	2
	1
	1

no smoking

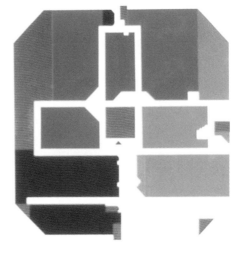

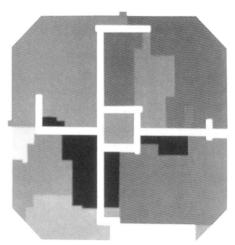

Above: The scale of the pylons was tested the old-fashioned way, before computer renderings. We took the mock-up for a walk down to the Charles River to be photographed in the open space.

Designer Coco Raynes
Architect Rogers, Butler & Burgun
Designed 1975

University of Wisconsin Clinical Science Center Madison, Wisconsin

The 2-million-square-foot teaching and medical facility was designed on a modular system, which resulted in a maze of identical spaces, without any clue to the outside world. Therefore the orientation completely relied on the signage.

We first traced the circulation routes along each floor—like a main avenue—and then actually attached the coded color stripes to the walls.

It became a modular system with end plugs, corners pieces, and directional units, accompanying patients and visitors along the corridors, from module to module.

Designer
Coco Raynes

Designed
1978

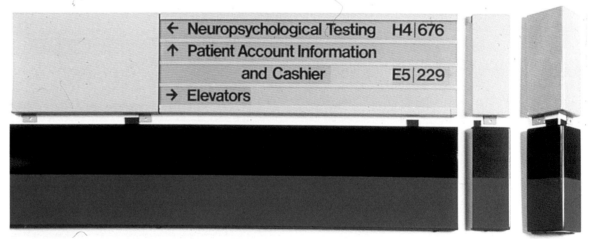

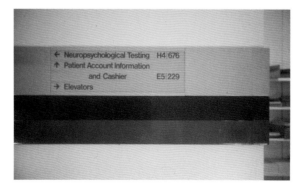

ENTERING

E5

Admissions
Patient Account Information
and Cashier
Pharmacy

A complex grid was designed for the overhead signs, informing the visitor which modules were being exited and entered.

Created by my office, the innovative insert system was the first of its kind. The listings featured a magnetic backing to facilitate future changes and additions.

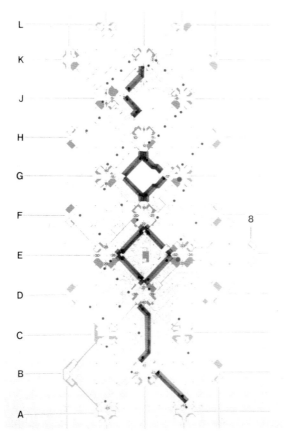

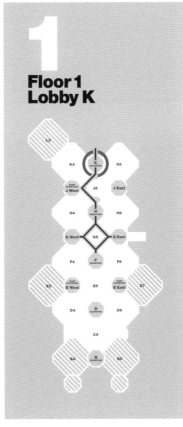

1

Floor 1
Lobby K

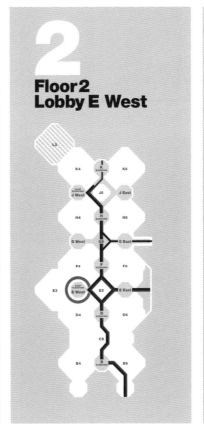

2

Floor 2
Lobby E West

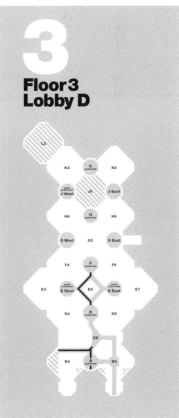

3

Floor 3
Lobby D

Joslin Diabetes Foundation
Boston, Massachusetts

The color scheme was adapted to the transparent building, and extended to the street façade as a welcome. A color harmony of ochres provided vibrant surroundings in high-traffic areas, while more subdued colors lead into quieter spaces. With the natural flow of traffic facilitated by the architectural design, the directional sign system blended with the interiors with minimal intrusion, while in contrast, the stairs, elevators, and exits were boldly identified to create a graphic element, and increase safety.

Photography: courtesy Payette/Nick Wheeler

Photography: courtesy Payette/Nick Wheeler

Photography: courtesy Payette/Nick Wheeler

Client
Joslin Diabetes Foundation

Architect
Payette
Tom Payette, FAIA

Designer
Coco Raynes

Completed
1974

Photography: Bill Miles, Boston

The client expected 500 donor names in the main lobby. Instead of the traditional plaques, we presented a design that incorporated the donor names, the history of the foundation, some of its artifacts, and the new building dedication. The mural was designed on a modular system of aluminum panels, with blank plaques for possible additions.

Previously unknown to the public, the handwritten text on the wall is an enlargement of a paper scrap from a notebook which witnessed the discovery of insulin by Charles Best and Frederick Banting (the latter sharing the 1923 Nobel Prize with John Macleod); they dedicated this note to Dr. Elliott Joslin in the margin.

Photography: Bill Miles, Boston

Avianca Colombian Airlines
Bogotá, Colombia

The bold lettering exuberantly celebrated the first Boeing 747 added to the fleet. The slanted letters, designed to depart from the traditional horizontal markings, traced the flow of air over the fuselage.

Client Avianca Colombian Airlines

Designer Coco Raynes

Completed 1975

Anato

Originally designed for Avianca, this logo combined
the letter "A" with an image of the proud eagle of the Andes.

At a later date, it became the logo for Anato, the Asociación
Colombiana de Agencias de Viajes y Turismo.

Designer Coco Raynes
Completed 1975

Harvest Restaurant

The logo evoked provincial cooking with seasonal ingredients.

Client/architect
Benjamin Thompson Associates
Cambridge, Massachusetts

Designer
Coco Raynes

Easy Street

The restaurant was designed in the art deco style, and the logo echoes the traditional decorative elements of that period.

Designer
Coco Raynes

easy street

Brambles

New bar and restaurant for Howard Johnson

Designer
Coco Raynes

Carlson Group
Commercial Real Estate

Douglass Kiene Inc.
Architects

Amaprop Development Inc.
Real Estate Company

douglass·kiene

Trail Blazers
Basketball team, Portland, Oregon

Client Frank Glickman, Inc.

Counterproductions, Inc.
Film and television production

Quik Pak
Self-packaging solutions

EDC|SSP
Social studies program for the EDC

Year-at-a-Glance Calendar

I designed the Year-at-a-Glance calendar to fit on a door (everyone has a door). This way the calendar would not be misplaced.

It became the office New Year gift for several decades, with special versions for the Israeli airline EL AL and Aviatur in South America.

Designer Coco Raynes

Designed 1976

Modular Giant Puzzle

One Piece Fits All. This giant puzzle was designed on a modular format. It allows any two pieces to fit together in any position. This avoids frustration for the child and encourages creativity, as new patterns can be endlessly created.

Designer Coco Raynes
Designed 1971

American
Corporate Identity
1989

The Best in
Environmental Graphics
Print Casebooks 7, 1987/1988

Awards of Excellence 1980, 1983, 1985
Art Directors Club of Boston

The Best in Environmental Graphics 1987, 1988
Print Casebook

1980s

In time, the nature of the projects changed. I wanted to distance myself from the work that hospital administrations continued to expect. My design work was considered very successful, but because of this recognition there was the danger of falling into easy repetition, into routines of little creative effort. Instead, the studio took a different approach to signage design, it adopted the metaphor of the "chameleon"—being there, informing, guiding and helping, but discreetly and in non-intrusive ways. The incentives for choosing materials and finishes, in close collaboration with the architect, came from the qualitative essence and sensitivity of the building's design.

As a rule, the signage had to reflect the client's identity and corporate philosophy. This was valid for both the corporate nature of signage for the world headquarters of Black & Decker, representing their industries and technology, as well as for the refined environment and hospitality services of New York's St. Regis Hotel.

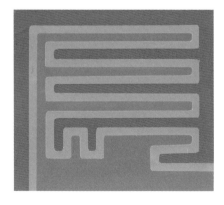

MIT Computer Lab
Cambridge, Massachusetts

Based on old computer parts, giant, decorative panels were manufactured in vandal-proof porcelain enamel to decorate the empty corridors.

Designer Coco Raynes
Completed 1980

MIT Computer Lab
Cambridge, Massachusetts

Articles highlighting the major achievements of the
computer lab were assembled to create a single,
large newspaper as a mural, placed in the reception area.

Designer Coco Raynes

Completed 1980

Ruggles Street MBTA Station
Boston, Massachusetts
Exhibit Display

The MBTA had the tradition of using displays along the platforms to show images of current neighborhood landmarks above the station.

These displays were situated throughout the concourse. At the time, Ruggles Street MBTA Station was in a neglected area. Therefore, I decided to focus on the past instead of the present, and traced the history and heritage of the Roxbury area across three centuries.

Client
Massachusetts Bay
Transportation Authority

Designer
Coco Raynes

Research
Lisa Grunwald

Architect
Stull Associates, Inc.
David Lee, FAIA

Completed
1981

Black & Decker Corporate World Headquarters
Towson, Maryland
Signage and Exhibit Design

Signage designer Coco Raynes
Architect FABRAP, Atlanta, Georgia
Completed 1982

The comprehensive signage system (incorporating the pre-existing company logo) for the headquarters complex guides and informs visitors from nearby highways and roads toward the site, parking areas, buildings, and corporate departments.

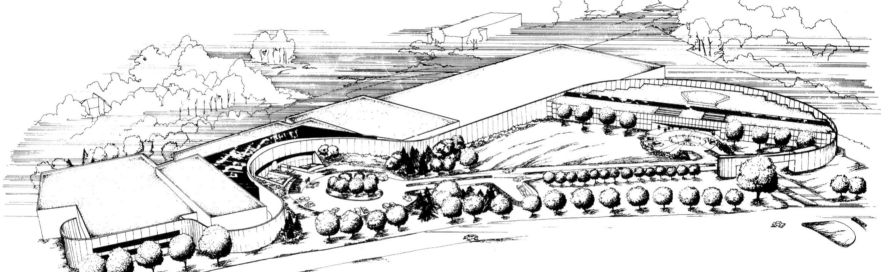

Employee Parking
Entrances 1,2,3,4
Entrances 2a,5
Service Entrances

Entrances 1,2,3,4
North Parking
Visitor Parking

West Parking

Service Entrances
Entrances 2a,5

STOP

EXIT

Entrances 2A,5
Service Entrances

West Parking

Above: The scale of the pylons was tested with full-size mock-ups along the road.

The exterior pylons are made of extruded aluminum with radius sides that harmonize with the finish and design of the curved façade. The design is now a product adopted by many manufacturers in the sign industry.

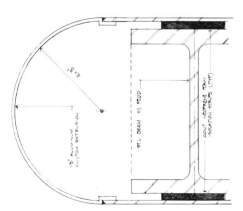

Black & Decker U.S. Inc.

Black & Decker Manufacturing Co.

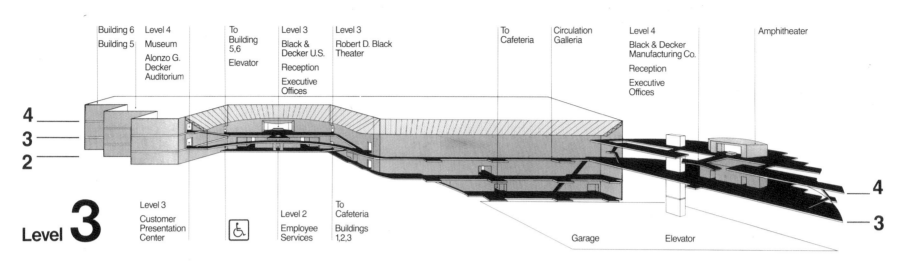

Building 6
Building 5

Level 4
Museum
Alonzo G.
Decker
Auditorium

To
Building
5,6
Elevator

Level 3
Black &
Decker U.S.
Reception
Executive
Offices

Level 3
Robert D. Black
Theater

To
Cafeteria

Circulation
Galleria

Level 4
Black & Decker
Manufacturing Co.
Reception
Executive
Offices

Amphitheater

Level **3**

Level 3
Customer
Presentation
Center

Level 2
Employee
Services

To
Cafeteria
Buildings
1,2,3

Garage

Elevator

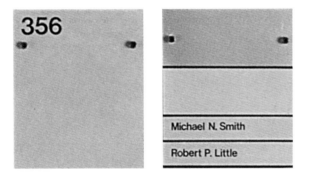

356

Michael N. Smith

Robert P. Little

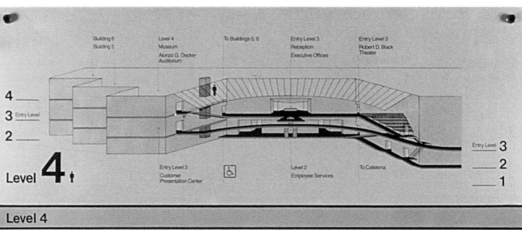

Building 6
Building 5

Level 4
Museum
Alonzo G. Decker
Auditorium

To Buildings 5, 6

Entry Level 3
Reception
Executive Offices

Entry Level 3
Robert D. Black
Theater

Level **4**

Entry Level 3
Customer
Presentation Center

Level 2
Employee Services

To Cafeteria

Level 4		
Alonzo G. Decker Auditorium		←
Museum		←
Buildings 5,6		←
Level 3		
Black and Decker U. S. Reception		
Customer Presentation Center		
Robert D. Black Theater		
Level 2		
Employee Services		
Level 1		
Cafeteria	via level 2	
Personnel	000	→

Interior Sign System

Printed aluminum inserts slide into an extruded rubber backing. Both materials and the fastening bolts echo the look of Black & Decker tools.

We wanted the client to be independent of sign manufacturers and to update the changes and additions inhouse. The rubber backing was kept in stock, and the aluminum inserts could be produced by Black & Decker's own graphic design department.

Display Kiosks and Pedestals

Our vision was for an "ongoing museum." As new inventions become history, the displays will continue to expand along the galleries and stair landings, where most of the traffic occurs.

The kiosks are internally illuminated and divided by a two-sided monolith printed with drawings and fragments of history, such as the cordless drill that was invented for the Apollo 11 flight and first moon landing in order to bring back geological core samples.

Tools are suspended behind the curved glass windows in front of their technical drawings.

Extra-large tools are displayed on gray pedestals, with lacquered burgundy sides. Some of them have clear acrylic tops to protect fragile documents.

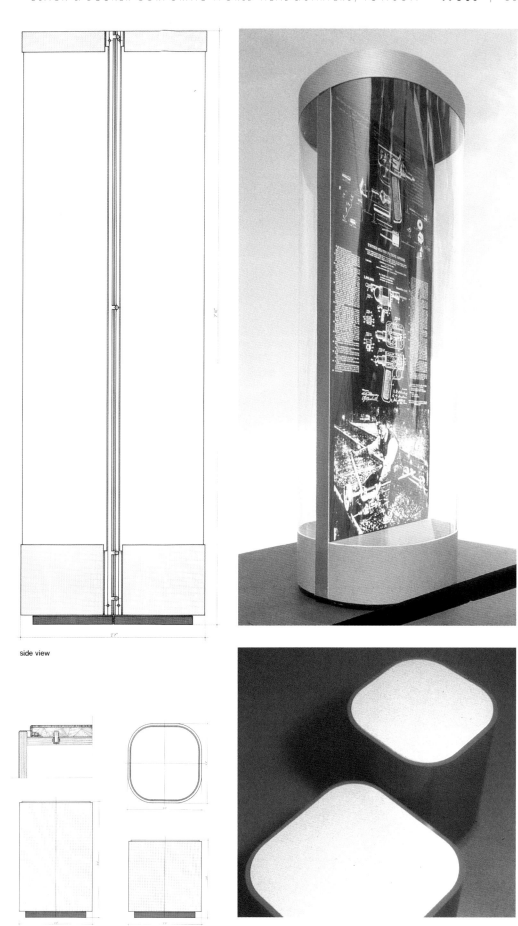

side view

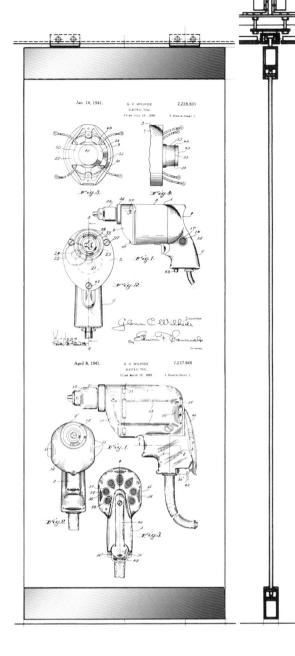

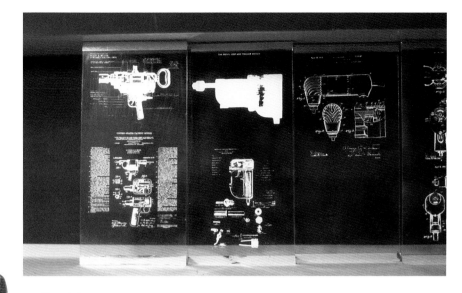

Exhibit designers
Coco Raynes
Sava Sveck

Drill Exhibit

Designed for the reception area, this exhibit prominently presents the tools. The display panels are made of glass with aluminum attachment details. The drills are secured in front of their specific technical drawings, with a special mounting device—a clear acrylic rod and an adjustable guard.

History and Tool Museum

The heart of the museum is in the multifunction auditorium, where Black & Decker's first 50 years are celebrated with documents, photos, and graphics; weaving history with technical achievements, such as the first hand drill, the women replacing men during the war, and the first corporate airplane.

The graphic display is laminated on the glass panels. It includes black-and-white and color photographs, letters, patent drawings, and other documents. The panels are 10 feet tall, 4 feet wide, and 3/4 inch thick. A special footing and attachment in brushed anodized aluminum were engineered to allow the glass panels to move on a suspended tracks.

The grid configuration permits the panels to be rearranged, either to seclude an area or divide the auditorium. For large functions, the panels can be lined up against the walls.

LOULOU'S
Boston, Massachusetts

The corporate images for this take-out rotisserie conveyed the care and quality of home cooking.

Designer
Coco Raynes

Completed
1986

Cave Atlantique
Boston, Massachusetts

The logo for this wine specialty store alludes to the wine pouring and was designed to be compatible with the neon technique.

Designer Coco Raynes

Client Amaprop Developments Inc.

Completed 1982

Photography: Steve Rosenthal

Product photography: J. Sherer

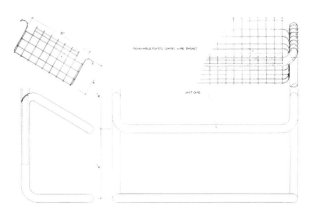

Au Bon Pain Prototype Store at Harvard Square

To eliminate the sad look of empty shelves at the end of the day, we presented a creative solution: displaying the bread and croissants in front of their own giant images. In addition to the large-scale photographs, a system of white baskets in tubular brass holders was designed to hold the baked goods.

Designer Coco Raynes

Architect Todd Lee Associates, Inc.

Completed 1984

Planet Coffee
High Street, Boston

Designers Coco Raynes, Kevin Sheehan
Completed 1983

Union College Food Court
Schenectady, New York

Designer Coco Raynes
Completed 1987

399 Boylston Street, Boston, Massachusetts

The project was a rare opportunity to design a façade identity before the building was completed. It meant having a perfectly integrated sign, metaphorically born with the building.

Three large-scale acrylic numerals were attached directly to the glass curtain. We had worked with extreme precision—the glass panels had been manufactured with the holes already in position, ready to receive the mounting pins.

Client
Boylston Associates

Architect
CBT Architects
Richard Bertman, FAIA

Designers
Coco Raynes
Sava Sveck

Completed
1983

550 North Reo
Tampa, Florida

The visual identity and the address of the office complex merged into one monumental sculpture, evoking the seaside location.

Client
Amaprop

Designer
Coco Raynes

Completed
1984

Photography: Jean M. Smith

931
Massachusetts Avenue
Cambridge

This work showcases the visual identity of the luxury condominium building.

Designer Coco Raynes

Client Amaprop

Completed 1984

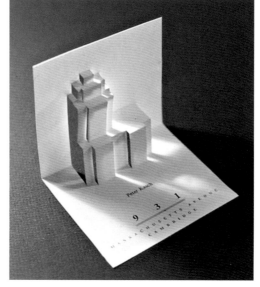

Photography: Jean M. Smith

Warren Chambers
419 Boylston Street, Boston

An address plaque and a directory were requested for the imposing old building listed on the Boston Historical Registry.

The signs appear as if they had always been there: the bronze directory frame duplicates the molding of the marble arch in reverse, and the exterior plaque indicates the street number with proper restraint.

Designer Coco Raynes
Architect CBT Architects
Completed 1983

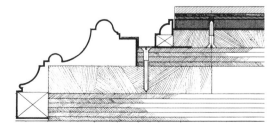

University Place at MIT
Cambridge, Massachusetts

Designer Coco Raynes

Architect Koetter | Kim & Associates

Designed 1984

This project was a great experience. The architect had no pre-conceived ideas regarding the nature of the signage design—the only expectation was perfection. This "carte blanche" resulted in our creation of our first glass sign, an innovative approach at the time (when signage was an afterthough made of plastic). The text is carved on the back surface and illuminated from the cove light above.

This was in 1984, many years before the ADA codes. Braille was not necessary, which was a good thing in this case; finding a manufacturer willing to work with glass carving had been difficult enough. Lasers were not yet used for signage.

The generic elevator call button plaques were replaced with precisely engineered stainless steel plates, engraved with the fire exit diagrams and safety regulations. This single-plaque approach eliminated the usual proliferation of signs.

Photography: Bill Miles, Boston

ITT Hartford Group Headquarters
Hartford, Connecticut

From the garage, the elevator bank does not connect to one of the towers. Visitors were directed to take the escalator to the main lobby, then board the corresponding elevator.

The neon diagram screams for attention and illustrates the tower's vertical circulation.

Designers Coco Raynes, Kevin Sheehan

Architect SLAM

Completed 1989

Photography: Bill Miles, Boston

City Square Park
Charlestown, Massachusetts

The curved information tables illustrate excavation artifacts and life in the historic town, complementing the landscape architect's exhibit, which presents the plan of the first large house in Charlestown. We marked the positions of the original posts with coins and seals.

Designer Coco Raynes

Landscape architect Halvorson Design Partnership, Inc.

Completed 1983

Boott Mills Canalways
Lowell, Massachusetts

The information diagram depicts the loop around the canalways. Used on all signage, it also serves as the trail's logo.

Designer Coco Raynes

Designed 1987

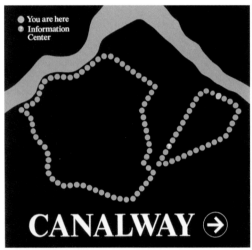

A custom attachment ring was originally designed to be used vertically on sign posts or horizontally along the canalway railings. With a simple rotation, the signs could be installed at the viewing height suitable for children or wheelchair users.

The rings for the railings were further engineered to the highest standards for maximum strength and durability.

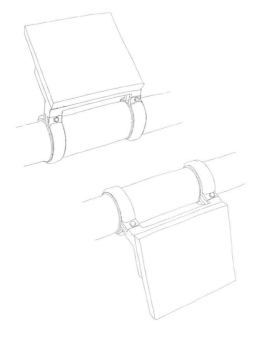

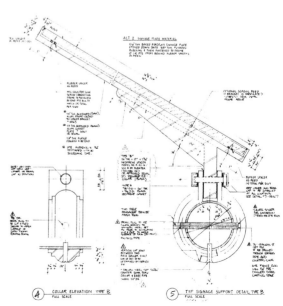

The St. Regis New York
New York City

Client
ITT Sheraton
Lynn MacMurtry, Director of Design

Designers
Coco Raynes
Kevin Shehan

Completed
1988

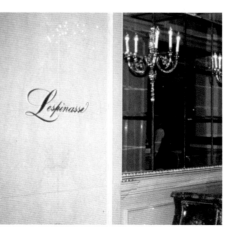

ITT Sheraton Manhattan Hotel
New York City

Designers
Coco Raynes
Kevin Sheehan

Completed
1988

ITT Sheraton New York Hotel and Towers New York City

Client ITT Sheraton

Designer Coco Raynes

Completed 1988

Photography: Bill Miles, Boston

Photography: Bill Miles, Boston

Photography: Bill Miles, Boston

Construction Fence

A construction fence was required during the hotel's renovation.

A great opportunity to advertise, but differently: instead of professional models, we invited the actual hotel staff to appear, wearing their uniforms and with the tools of their trade.

It was a genuine smiling success!

Sheraton Inn Fredericton
New Brunswick, Canada

The signs and logos reflect a very conservative look, mixing script, brass, and mahogany, to accompany the hotel interiors designed as an "old inn in the country."

Designers Coco Raynes, Kevin Shehan
Completed 1988

Swissôtel The Bosphorus
Istanbul, Turkey

Borrowing from the floor adornment detail, the signage is made of green marble and brass.

Logos were designed for all the retail stores, bars and restaurants, and like the signage, they mix marble and brass in their applications.

Packaging and hotel amenities feature the logos while respecting the Swissôtel graphic standards.

Designers Coco Raynes, Kevin Shehan
Completed 1989

Dragon Valley Hotel
South Korea

Designer Coco Raynes

Completed 1989

One Brattle Square
Cambridge, Massachusetts

Designers   Coco Raynes, Kevin Shehan
Completed   1989

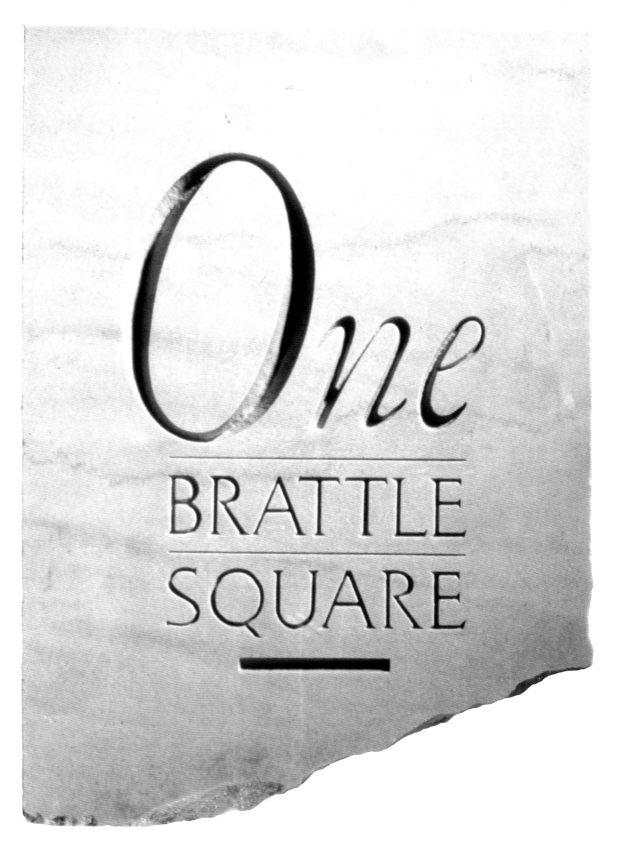

depot

Depot

Visual Identity for a stationery and
office supply company with warehouses,
outlets, and a truck fleet.

Client Depot Stationers, NY
Design completed 1985

Opposite:
Johnson & Johnson
Catalog for the firm's Orthopaedic Division.

Design completed 1990

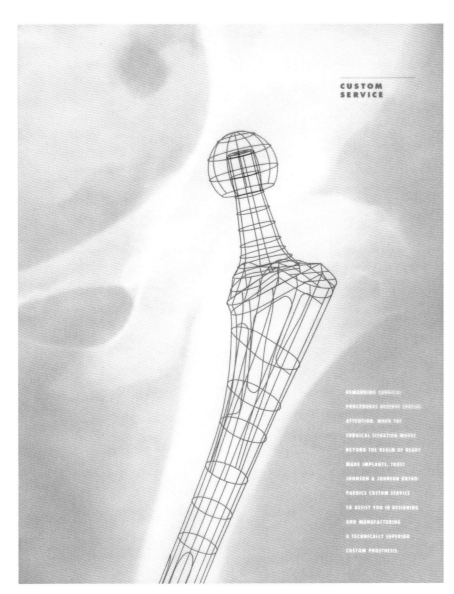

CUSTOM
SERVICE

DEMANDING SURGICAL
PROCEDURES DESERVE SPECIAL
ATTENTION. WHEN THE
SURGICAL SITUATION MOVES
BEYOND THE REALM OF READY
MADE IMPLANTS, TRUST
JOHNSON & JOHNSON ORTHO-
PAEDICS CUSTOM SERVICE
TO ASSIST YOU IN DESIGNING
AND MANUFACTURING
A TECHNICALLY SUPERIOR
CUSTOM PROSTHESIS.

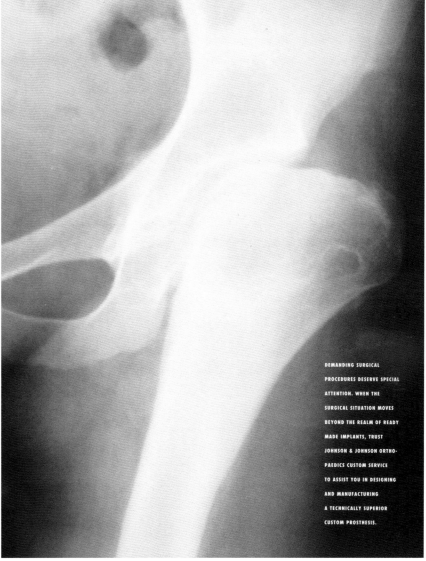

DEMANDING SURGICAL
PROCEDURES DESERVE SPECIAL
ATTENTION. WHEN THE
SURGICAL SITUATION MOVES
BEYOND THE REALM OF READY
MADE IMPLANTS, TRUST
JOHNSON & JOHNSON ORTHO-
PAEDICS CUSTOM SERVICE
TO ASSIST YOU IN DESIGNING
AND MANUFACTURING
A TECHNICALLY SUPERIOR
CUSTOM PROSTHESIS.

Johnson & Johnson
ORTHOPAEDICS

CUSTOM SERVICE

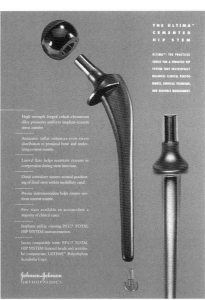

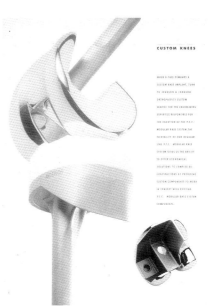

"We can no longer have the arrogance to design for a select group, and in the near future, it is my belief that Universal Design will be the norm. An elegant inclusive information system is often developed at the same cost as a mediocre, non-inclusive one." — Coco Raynes

From acceptance remarks IDSA (Industrial Designers Society of America)
Gold Award 1994

Back in 1973, my first healthcare client had been the Massachusetts Eye and Ear Infirmary in Boston. At that time, I had suggested to place Braille messages behind the existing handrails in corridors, stairways, and elevators. The concept was dismissed as a gimmick.

In 1988, in view of the impending enforcement of regulations established in the Americans with Disabilities Act (ADA), I decided that it was time to develop my concept of a comprehensive and fully functioning Braille Handrail System into a product for museums, airports, transit stations, and public buildings. How could we be satisfied with Braille by the door yet provide no means to get to the door or to any other location? I was not interested in the superficial pretence of the "minimum requirements" defined by the ADA.

BusinessWeek 1997
Industrial Design Excellence Awards

Honor Award 1994
Society of Environmental Graphic Design

1990s

My handrail design created the missing links between all functions of a building—from entrances, exits, desired locations, and services, to specific objects—thereby opening up any space for total inclusion and interaction. The multisensory program was soon followed by tactile representations of drawings, paintings, sculptures, and maps on glass.

This work led us to open several national museums to blind visitors in France and Latin America. The highly published, innovative programs were influential and became valuable both socially and culturally, forging the "right to equal information" into law in France. We had proven that intellectual accessibility was possible—and our design had made a difference.

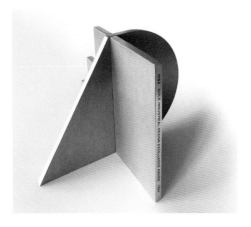

IDSA (Industrial Designers Society of America)
Gold Award

SEGD (Society for Environmental Graphic Design)
Honor Award

ID (International Design Magazine)
Award of Excellence and Innovation

AIAR (American Institute of Architectural Research)
Merit Award

Raynes Rail
Braille and Audio
Handrail System

*Case Study at the Massachusetts
Eye and Ear Infirmary*
Boston, Massachusetts

Despite the first ADA regulations in 1990, the visually impaired visitors still faced great obstacles in orienting themselves in unknown surroundings.

The regulations outlined requirements such as Braille, tactile letters, contrast values, and specific mounting heights for all identification signage. However, just finding these signs amid walls containing pictures, lighting fixtures, and interrupted floor patterns remained a challenge. It is unreasonable to expect a blind traveler to feel one's way along a corridor, trying to obtain directional information.

In order to develop and test the concept, a formal study needed to be conducted. The Massachusetts Eye and Ear Infirmary was the obvious choice. Two floors with the largest number of eye patients were designated to build the case study. With the assistance of the Vice President, Joseph Castellana, an exceptional team of Braille consultants was assembled, including representatives from the Carroll Center for the Blind and from the Massachusetts Commission for the Blind.

The installations were tested over a couple of months and, with the consultants' help, a specific and precise vocabulary was developed to give directions along the handrails.

"This is problem solving of a high order, and effectively broadens our interpretation and visual communications."

—Jury, 100th Show
 American Center for Design

"I knew where I was. It was almost like seeing again."

—Charles H. Crawford, Commissioner
 Massachusetts Commission for the Blind

"The blind person can travel within complex buildings with independence and ease."

—Arthur O'Neill
 *Director of Education
 Carroll Center for the Blind*

"Congratulations on the acclaim you received for developing such a wonderful tool as the Raynes Rail.

... We are interested in learning more about your system and encouraging its installation at locations throughout Wisconsin."

—Mark J. Karstedt
 *Director of Development
 & Public Relations
 Wisconsin Council of the Blind, Inc.*

Patents

5,284,444
5,366,050
5,417,574
D 353,455
D 353,467

Above and right: **Earthplace, Connecticut** Installations along walking trails, with poem excerpts in Braille

Opposite: **Cooper Hewitt Museum, New York** Installation of handrail with audio commentaries system

Photography: Bill Miles, Boston

Combined Jewish
Philanthropies Headquarters

Following the Raynes Rail success, I wanted to develop aesthetic
and refined solutions for accessibility. The first step was to revisit
the glass signage designed in 1984—this time with Braille raised
from the blasted surface. This was our second glass sign design
and the first glass sign ever with Braille. Extremely difficult to get
manufactured: nobody wanted touch it!

Designer Coco Raynes
Completed 1994

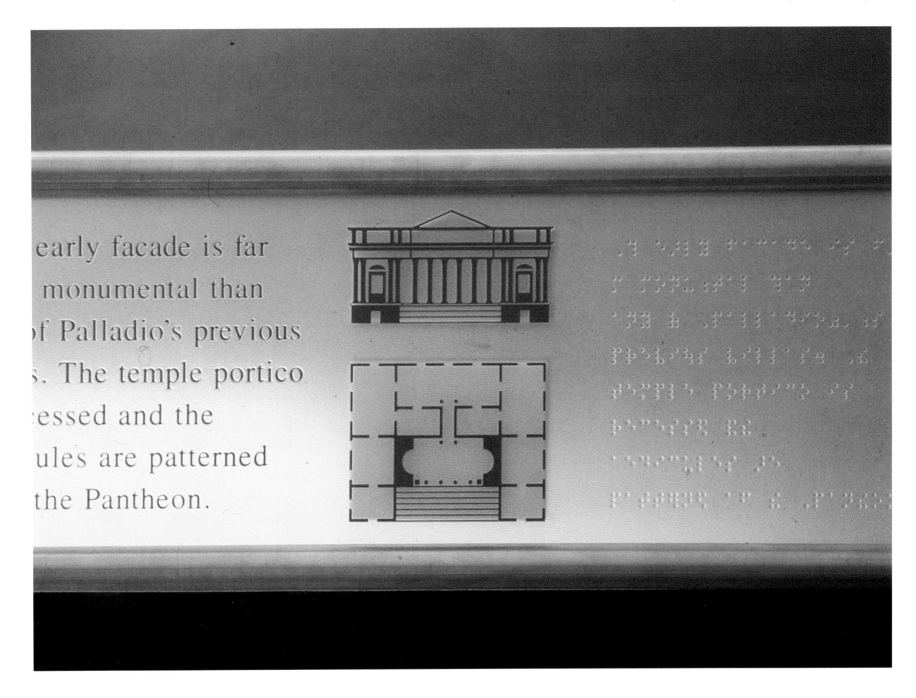

Raynes Rail (Glass Prototype)

The next step was to create a slanted glass railing for exhibit displays with Braille and raised drawings. The clear glass permitted the application of color to the second surface, without the risk of being scratched by users.

I was now ready to make the most refined buildings ADA-compliant and address exhibits beyond the minimum requirements.

Designer   Coco Raynes
Completed   1994

"The Museum at Your Fingertips" is a tactile itinerary through several museums in northern France, where blind visitors can discover the museums' collections of art and architecture across several centuries.

The examples of tactile itineraries presented in the next pages might, at first, seem systematic or repetitive. However, each art collection varied significantly, and each museum comprised its own specific architecture, rules, and requirements. Throughout the process and dealing with these challenges, my design vocabulary for opening the museums to blind visitors evolved with each project and went a little further each time. The goal was to allow the blind person to navigate the spaces independently, without the need of a guide or special appointment.

Clients

Ministère de la Culture, Département des Musées de France
Claude Gilbert, Chargée de Mission (Project Manager)

Fédération du Nord du Pas de Calais "Le Musée au bout des doigts"
Jaqueline Spriet, Presidente (President)

Musée des Beaux-Arts et de la Dentelle, Calais
The entire bronze collection was assembled in one single gallery and could be touched by visitors, including the original studies from Auguste Rodin and Antoine Bourdelle. We were given the responsibility to renovate the gallery and create a new, accessible museography.

Musée des Beaux-Arts, Arras
Only a few examples of medieval art could be touched by visitors, and these pieces were disseminated across several galleries. The existing museography could not be changed.

Musée des Beaux-Arts, Valenciennes
Creation of a tactile itinerary throughout the spaces devoted to the sixteeenth through twentieth centuries (XVIe au XXe Siècle Gallerie), where the existing signage and none of the museography could be modified. The "invisible" itinerary used at least one example of each representative period, with statues distributed throughout the five galleries. It continued to the workshops, library, and facilities located on the lower level.

Musée de la Chartreuse de Douai
The multisensory exhibits present the carvings of medieval sarcophagi and the evolution of religious ornamental architecture in an original 1663 monastery and chapel completed in 1725.

Musée des Beaux-Arts et de la Dentelle Calais, France

Inside the nineteenth-century sculpture room blind visitors can touch the collections, including masterpieces by Antoine Bourdelle and Auguste Rodin. Our task was to renovate the gallery and to create an inclusive visit with an multisensory information system.

The new museography—with its simplified floor plan and only two rows of statues—can be easily memorized. The space between the pedestals allows for easy circumvolution by visitors in wheelchairs or with seeing-eye dogs.

Exhibits are divided according to tactile and nontactile collections, isolating fragile pieces from the bronze sculptures, while respecting their chronological order. Large sculptures that cannot be touched are secluded, placed at the end of the gallery.

Designer
Coco Raynes

Completed
Phase 1 1997
Phase 2 1998

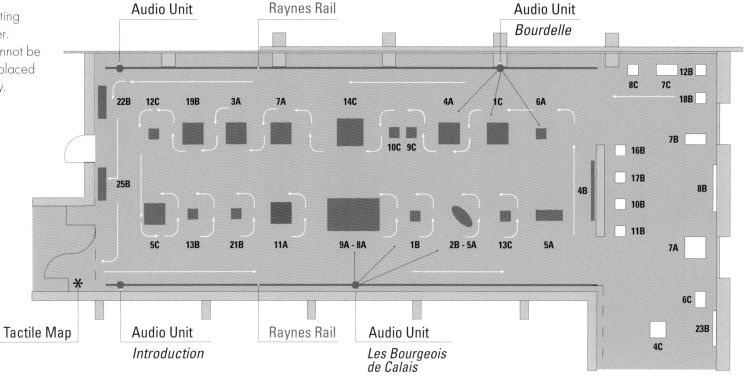

Auguste Rodin

Paris 1840 - Meudon 1917

Tête d'Eustache de Saint-Pierre
Etude pour le Monument
des Bourgeois de Calais - Vers 1886-1887

Bronze. Fonte E. Godard, 1981
Don des Amis du Musée de Calais, 1981
81.13.1

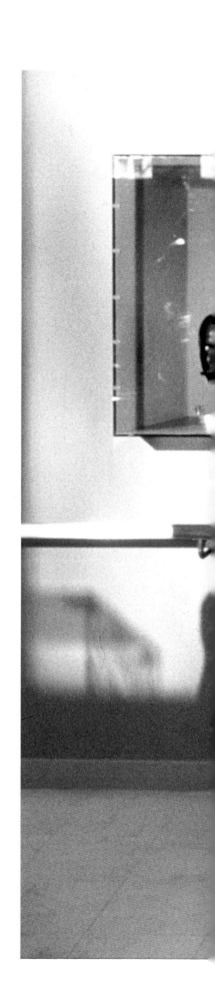

Minimalist display pedestals with adapted
heights were designed to be manufactured
by the museum's in-house carpenters.

They incorporate glass information panels
on a slanted surface. Braille and large
tactile text present the statues and describe
their characteristics.

Auguste Rodin
Paris 1840 - Meudon 1917

Les Bourgeois de Calais - 1885
Deuxième maquette pour le Monument.

Bronze, Fonte Susse, 1973
Dépôt du Musée Rodin, 1973
D.77.5.1

A handrail with Braille introduces each sculpture and gives its exact location in paces, directing blind visitors to the statues they wish to discover. Audio units along the rail, activated by photosensors, describe the sculptures' characteristics in several languages.

Musée des Beaux-Arts
Arras, France

Similar to the introduction of a book, the raised drawings introduce the statues and facilitate their tactile discovery.

Pedestals incorporate descriptive panels with text and Braille on black glass, which discretely blend with the existing signage.

Designer Coco Raynes
Completed 1997

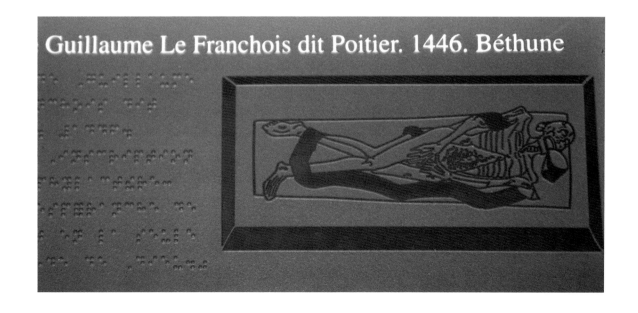

Guillaume Le Franchois dit Poitier. 1446. Béthune

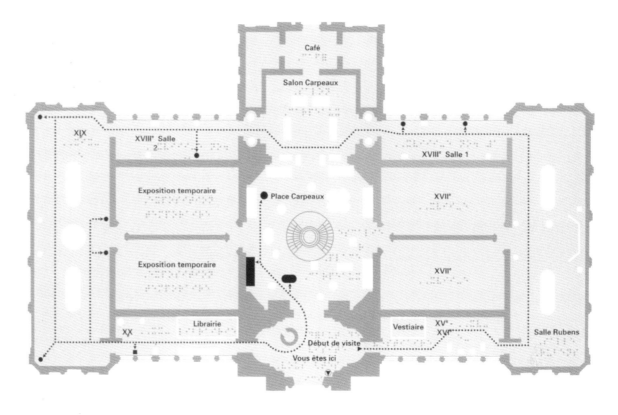

Musées des Beaux-Arts
Valenciennes, France

The museum requested an almost "invisible information system." The design could not interfere with existing signage, and furthermore, the museography could not be modified. We created a tactile itinerary within the existing museography, simple enough to be remembered, using at least one example of each representative period, with the exception of the fifteenth-century gallery where no art could be touched. The statues are distributed throughout the sixteenth- to twentieth-century galleries.

A main directory presents the itinerary with a raised map. Braille information on the inside of a rail segment provides directions and distances. Tactile maps are consistently located on the right side of entrances to indicate the path through the galleries. Braille information is incorporated into the pedestals with the addition of an etched glass surface. Raised dots (Tacdots) delineate the path on the floor in locations that are difficult to navigate. The dots have a distinctive sound when tapped.

Designer   Coco Raynes
Completed   1999

"C'est avec grand plaisir que je vous remercie pour la dernière installation que vous avez réalisée au musée des Beaux Arts de Valenciennes, dans le cadre de l'opération Le musée au bout des doigts. Tous les échos (---) que j'en ai reçus sont forts élogieux, et font état du plaisir de ces visiteurs pouvant, enfin, se considérer comme les autres.(---). De ce fait, nous allons, encore longtemps, nous pencher ensemble, sur des adaptations qui requièrent à chaque fois une solution originale puisque chaque musée a des spécificités dont il est fier."

Claude Gilbert
Ministère de la Culture
Départment des Musées de France

"It is with great pleasure that I thank you for the last installation you made at the Museum of Fine Arts in Valenciennes, as part of the program: The Museum at Your Fingertips. All the comments (—) that I have received are very eulogistic, and mention the pleasure of these visitors who can finally consider themselves as the others (—). As a result, we will work together for a long time on adaptations that each time require an original solution since each museum has specificities of which it is proud."

———————————

"Je tiens à vous remercier à nouveau pour les installations que vous avez réalisées afin d'équiper les musées à l'intention des aveugles et mal voyants.

Vous avez une large part dans le succès remporté par notre action « Le musée au bout des bout des doigts ». La qualité de votre travail dans les musées d'Arras, de Calais et de Valenciennes a été soulignée par le Ministre de la Culture, et leur efficacité a recueilli une adhésion unanime.

Il est dans nos intentions d'étendre notre action - comme prévu - à d'autres musées du Nord Pas-de-Calais: c'est vous dire que nous serons amenés sous peu à solliciter à nouveau votre compétence et votre dévouement."

J. Spriet, Présidente
Fédération du Nord de la France
des Sociétés d'Amis des Musées

"I want to thank you again for the facilities you have built to equip museums for the blind and visually impaired.

You have [played] a big part in the success of our program: "The Museum at Your Fingertips". The quality of your work in the museums of Arras, Calais, and Valenciennes was highlighted by the Minister of Culture, and their effectiveness received unanimous praise.

It is our intention to extend our program—as planned—to other museums in the Nord Pas-de-Calais: that is to say that we will soon be asking for your competence and your dedication again."

Musée de la Chartreuse
Douai, France

The museum was formerly a monastery. The tactile and accessible program was the opportunity to introduce the religious ornamental architecture of the sixteenth and seventeenth centuries to all of the public. The heavily adorned pilasters are represented by tactile drawings.

Designers Coco Raynes, Kate Blehar
Completed 2005

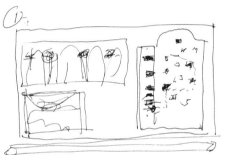

Multisensory displays are accompanied by audio commentary that recreates the monastic atmosphere.

Facsimiles of ornamental stones describe the adorned bases of the Gothic arches, bringing the carvings literally to one's fingertips.

Recumbent effigies, from 1161 to 1664, are harmoniously positioned in front of each window, with a descriptive tactile plaque on the sill to eliminate floor-mounted obstacles.

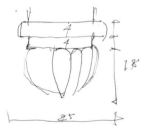

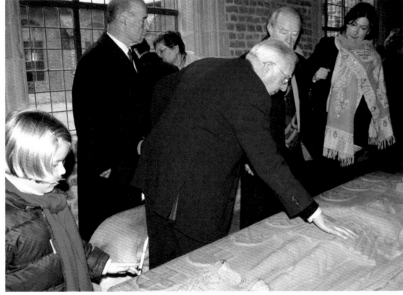

Dalle funéraire de Pierre Parr et Christine Boisot
1607. Le couvent des clarisses
Pierre bleue

CAROLUS, OFFICII MEMOR AC PIETATIS AVITAE, CENOBIARCHIA SUIS
POSUIT GENITORIBUS ISTA CHRISTINE BOISOT, PETRO PARR, AEDE
SEPULTIS MARMOREU(M) HOC GRATI MONUMENTUM PIGN(US) AMORIS

Museo Nacional de Colombia
Bogotá, Colombia

The National Museum of Colombia is housed in an ex-penitentiary built in 1823, now classified as an historic monument.

The collections, ranging from the Pre-Colombian era to the Spanish Conquest, to Contemporary art, were displayed on two floors and could not be touched.

At the request of the Secretary of Culture, I was asked to create the master plan for an educational program that would address all visitors, including children, visitors in wheelchairs, or those visually impaired.

The added museography had to complement the existing one, and blend with the Colonial Spanish architecture. The result was a multisensory itinerary that highlighted typical examples of each period with tactile orientation diagrams, raised drawings, facsimiles, and multilingual audio commentaries. This allowed for an autonomous experience within the general visit.

At the entrance of each gallery, a map introduces the floor plan, and a raised path leads to the multisensory exhibits. Once inside the gallery, the blind visitor navigates easily through the space by counting the columns.

Designer Coco Raynes
Completed 1999

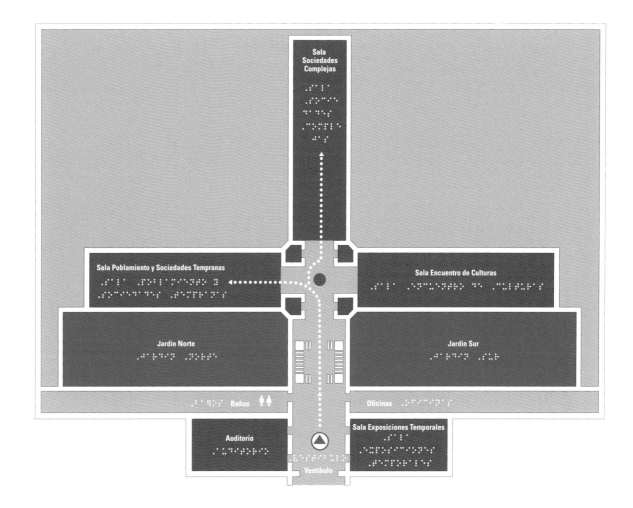

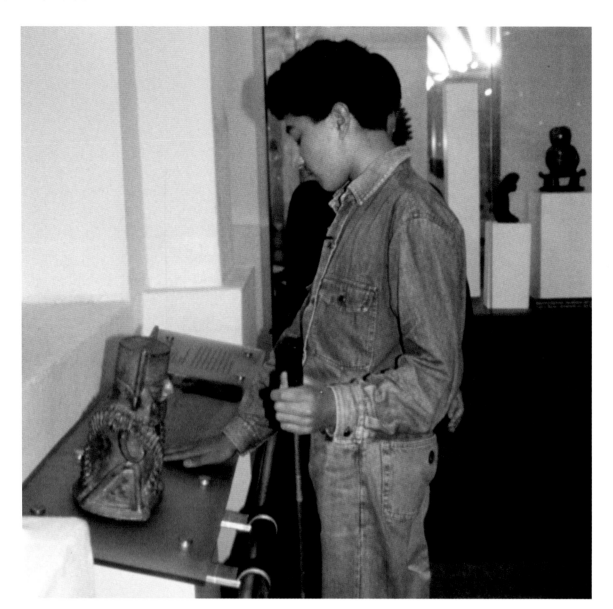

Lecterns with adapted height and slanted glass surfaces were fitted in the recesses of the existing archways.

A segment of the Braille-and-audio handrail protects the edge of the glass, and addresses all visitors.

Pre-Colombian replicas are displayed on the glass surface accompanied by a tactile drawing, Braille, raised text, and an audio commentary that describes the characteristics of each piece.

The original artifacts are exhibited in adjacent display cases.

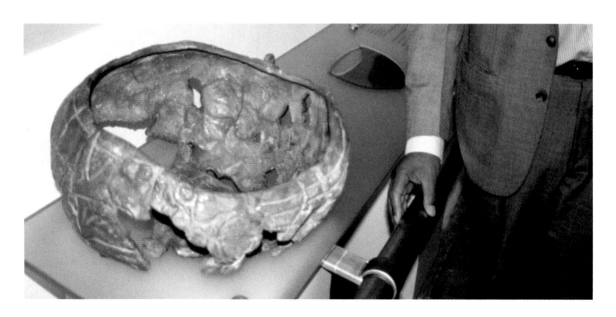

Two portraits of Simón Bolívar depict the young victorious general and the mature, defeated man. Tactile silhouettes translate the body language, and the audio system plays excerpts of Bolívar's journals from both periods.

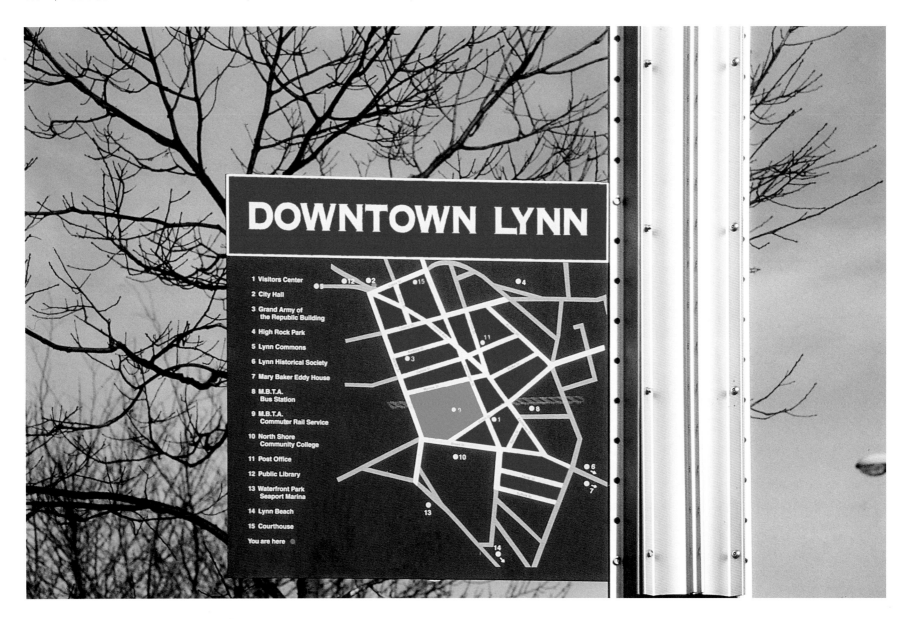

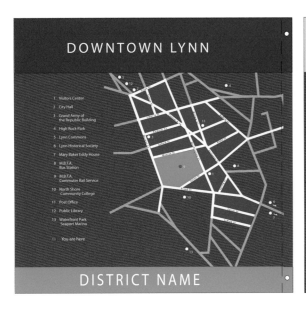

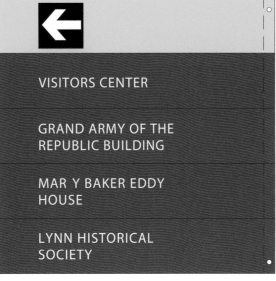

Downtown Lynn, Massachusetts

The irregular street angles needed an innovative solution that would allow signs to actually point in the direction of the streets. An attachment ring that could mirror the street layout was an intriguing idea to pursue.

A custom extrusion formed the desired attachment around the existing lampposts. It addresses the information needs of Downtown Lynn with orientation maps, street signs, directionals, and traffic regulations mounted at a variety of angles.

Designer   Coco Raynes
Completed   1993

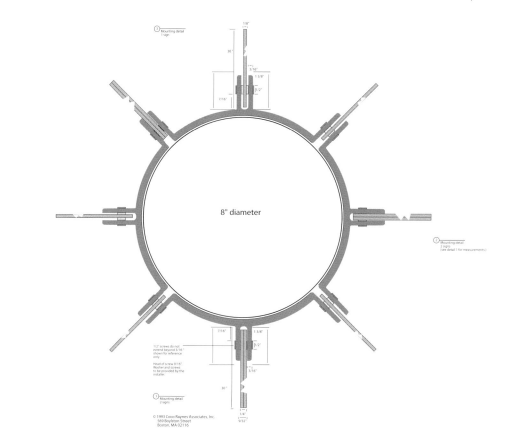

8" diameter

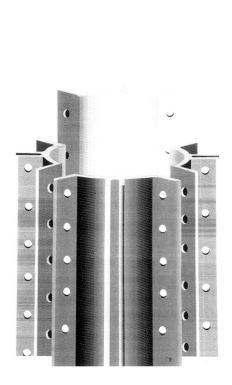

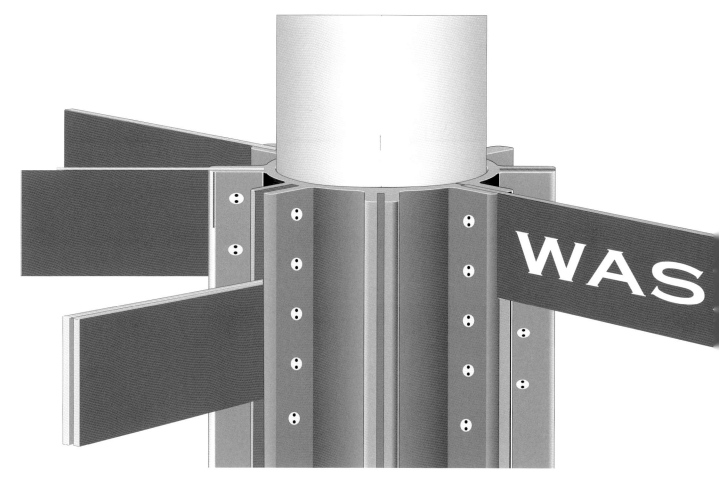

WAS

Boston Police Headquarters
Boston, Massachusetts

Simplicity was a must. The state seal and the modular information system are made of aluminum.

A color-coded edge reinforces the designations for the north and south wings throughout the building.

Designer
Coco Raynes

Architect
Stull and Lee

Completed
1998

PUBLIC SERVICE

← **CASHIER**   **NORTH ELEVATORS** →
INFORMATION

SOUTH WING ↑ **SOUTH ELEVATORS**

2
NORTH WING

N·261	AUTO SQUAD
N·264	BUREAU OF INVESTIGATIVE SERVICES
N·251	CONFERENCE ROOM
N·254	CONFERENCE ROOM
N·255	DOMESTIC VIOLENCE
N·262	EXERCISE ROOM
N·261	FUGITIVE SQUAD
N·259	HOMICIDE
N·258	INTELLIGENCE
N·261	INVESTIGATIVE PLANNING
N·257	SEXUAL ASSAULT
N·255	VICTIM ASSISTANCE

SOUTH WING

S·249	BALLISTICS
S·242	EVIDENCE STORAGE
S·243	LATENT FINGER PRINTS
S·248	PHOTOGRAPHY LAB

N·261

VIDEO ID
AUTO SQUAD
FUGITIVE SQUAD
INVESTIGATIVE PLANNING

N·158

CHILD CARE
CENTER

U.S. Post Office and Courthouse
Old San Juan, Puerto Rico

The decorative attachment links the glass signs to the historic building's original ironwork.

A specially designed magnetic system permits the listings and arrows to be changed.

Designer
Coco Raynes

Architect
Finegold Alexander Architects
Sherman "Pat" Morss Jr., AIA, LEED AP
Maurice Finegold, FAIA

Completed
1998

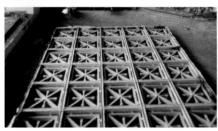

RESIDENT COMMISSIONER

U. S. POST OFFICE

ELEVATOR LOBBY

U. S. COURT ROOMS

1 11/16"
1/2"
1 11/16"
1/2"
1 11/16"
1/2"
1 11/16"
1/2"
1 11/16"
1/2"
1 11/16"
2 7/8"

16 1/2"

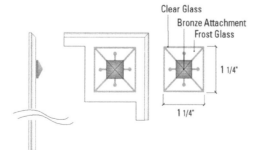

Clear Glass
Bronze Attachment
Frost Glass

1 1/4"

1 1/4"

4 Bronze Pyramid Attachment
Dark Bronze

BRONZE FRAME/INSERT

1 11/16"

1 11/16"

BRONZE FRAME

1/16" BRONZE LIP

MAGNETIC INSERT ALLOWS
ARROW TO POINT IN ANY DIRECTION

MAGNETIC INSERT
ETCHED AND PAINT FILLED BLACK

11/32"
9/32"
11/32"

3 MOVABLE DIRECTIONAL ARROW – **FOR FORMAT D SIGNS**
Dark Bronze - ARROW PAINTED BLACK

Temple Emanuel
Newton, Massachusetts

The signs are fabricated from porcelain tiles—an unusual material for signs. The design recalls the courtyard architecture and color. The blasted surface reveals raised text and Braille, as required by the ADA regulations.

Designer
Coco Raynes

Architect
Finegold Alexander Architects
Maurice Finegold, FAIA

Completed
1998

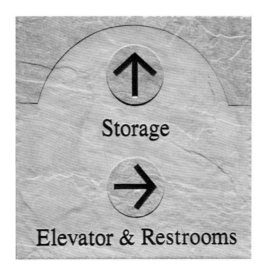

200 Newbury Street
Boston, Massachusetts

Sculptural aluminum letters emphasize the curved wall behind the reception desk.

The unusually long door signs are made of glass and they both provide information and protect the walls. The custom-made sign attachments are anchored to the metal batten strips.

Designer
Coco Raynes

Architect
CBT Architects
Richard Bertman, FAIA

Client
Sawyer Enterprises, Inc.

Completed
1998

This three-dimensional, two-sided parking sign was the result of a low-clearance situation: to compensate for the lack of height, the sign needed depth to appear substantial. Instead of the typical afterthought 'P' for parking, the sign is an industrial sculpture. In close collaboration with the architect, the attachment was designed as an extension of the building's ornamental details.

This innovative approach to parking identification was soon multiplied—by others—and appeared at every garage entrance in Boston.

Designer Coco Raynes
Completed 2005

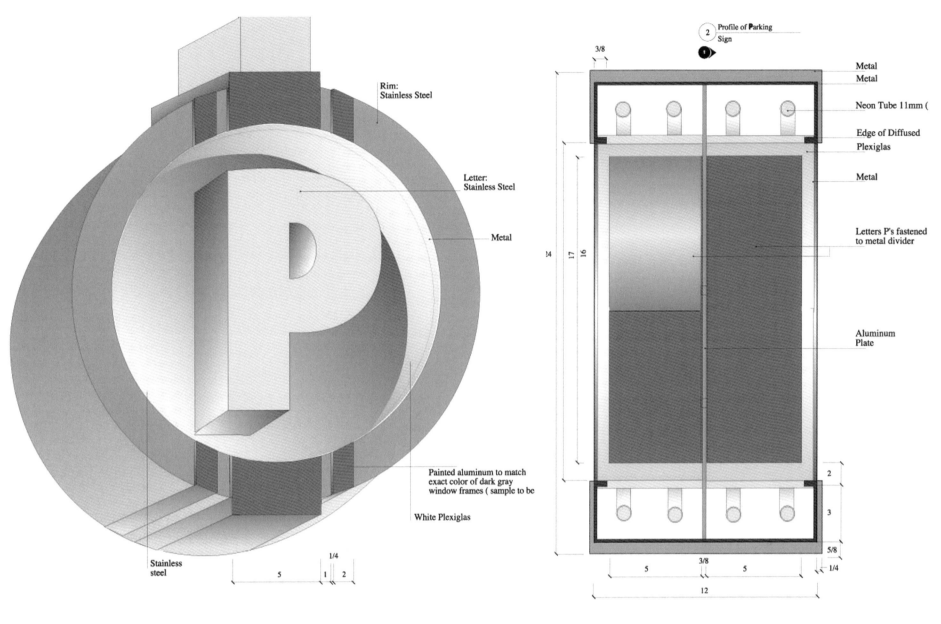

Rim:
Stainless Steel

Letter:
Stainless Steel

Metal

Painted aluminum to match
exact color of dark gray
window frames (sample to be

White Plexiglas

Stainless
steel

1/4

5   1   2

② Profile of **P**arking
Sign

3/8

Metal
Metal

Neon Tube 11mm (

Edge of Diffused
Plexiglas

Metal

Letters P's fastened
to metal divider

Aluminum
Plate

24   17   16

2

3

5/8

5   3/8   5   1/4

12

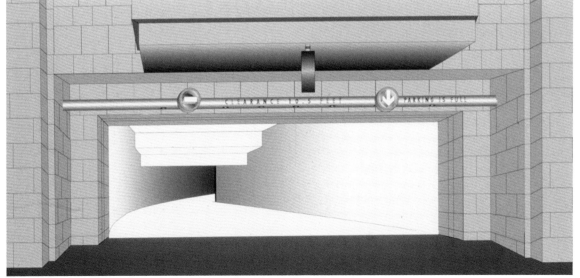

Maloka Interactive Museum
Bogotá, Colombia

I was invited to conduct a two-week-long charrette to lead the in-house graphic design department of the Maloka museum. A fabulous experience: everything was ready in two weeks, manufactured in one month, and installed before the opening!

The design matched the building architectural style, with no-frill attachments or fancy manufacturing techniques. Only economical and immediately available materials were used.

Designers Maloka Design Team, Coco Raynes

Client Ministerio de la Cultura

Completed 1998

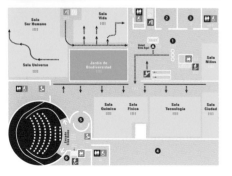

Maloka
Ciencia + Tecnología Interactiva

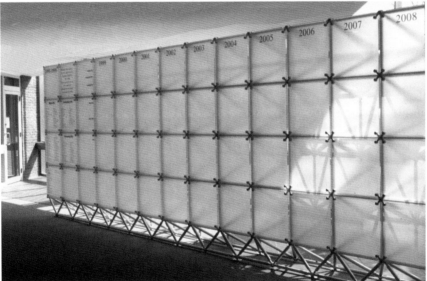

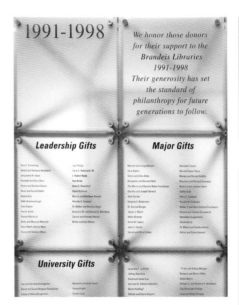

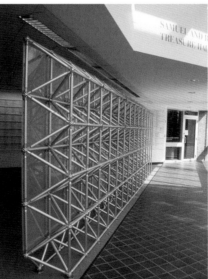

Brandeis University
Waltham, Massachusetts

Asked to design a donor recognition wall, I was surprised to find that there was no wall available to receive the names. Therefore we created our own freestanding structure, using an existing modular system. The new partition secludes a part of the lobby for private functions, and offers two display sides.

The donor names commenced in 1999 and the wall reached its maximum capacity in 2019. With donor names meticulously added every year, the design offered "peace of mind" to the university's administration for twenty years.

Designer Coco Raynes
Designed 1998
Completed 2018

"Design has no gender: there is only good design and bad design."
— Coco Raynes

From acceptance remarks BSA, Boston Society of Architects
Women in Design Award of Excellence 2006

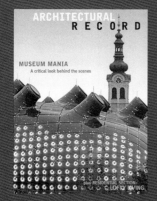

Excellence in Universal Design 2003
Adaptive Environments

Gold Award CLIO 2003

Honor Award 2002
Society of Environmental Graphic Design

Honor Award 2002
U.S. General Services Administration

2000s

As the office progressed in its quest for excellence—refining aesthetics and techniques to develop practical solutions for accessibility—we were invited to work on a very diverse range of projects, often multilingual and international.

I had never dreamed, however, that the Aeróports de Paris (ADP)—would ask me to create the prototypes for accessibility at Charles de Gaulle Airport.

The new decade brought with it projects that were so much more multi-faceted in scope and this diversity, coupled with the team's enthusiasm, stimulated our creativity.

Visual Identity
United States Access Board
National Competition
Award-Winning Design

Visual Identity for the Federal Agency
Committed to Accessible Design

Designers
Coco Raynes
Kate Blehar

Completed
2001

Official versions of the logo.
Lifting Barriers

We selected the star,
a symbol already identified
by all Braille readers.

In all elevators in the United
States, the star indicates
the floor that provides direct
access to the street.

The four stripes refer to
the four words of the title:
United States Access Board.

UNITED STATES ACCESS BOARD

Charles de Gaulle Airport
Paris, France
Inclusive Wayfinding and
Information System for
Terminal 2C

The firm was contacted by Aeróports de
Paris (ADP), France, to create a universally
accessible wayfinding and information
system. Terminal 2C at Charles de Gaulle
Airport, one of the largest international
airports in the world, was designated to
create the prototype.

The challenge was to direct passengers with
reduced mobility (PMR) from the point of
arrival on the sidewalk to the PMR reception
area within the terminal. Our concept
was approved because the proposed
components of the information system could
be integrated into the architectural design of
the new constructions or easily be retrofitted
into existing facilities. The visual, tactile, and
audio information is universally understood
and conveyed in three languages—French,
English, and Spanish.

An information table introduces the floor
plan of the overall terminal and orients
passengers with reduced mobility to the
reception area.

The tactile map indicates the paths,
counters, and reserved seating. At the
edge of the table, a Raynes Rail segment
protects the glass and further informs
travelers with audio messages.

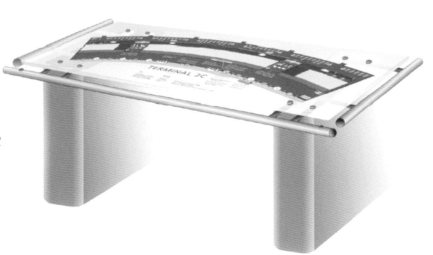

Client
Aeróports de Paris (ADP)

Designers
Coco Raynes
Kate Blehar

Awards
SEGD Honor Award 2002
IDSA Bronze Award 2003
CLIO Gold Award 2003

Completed
2002

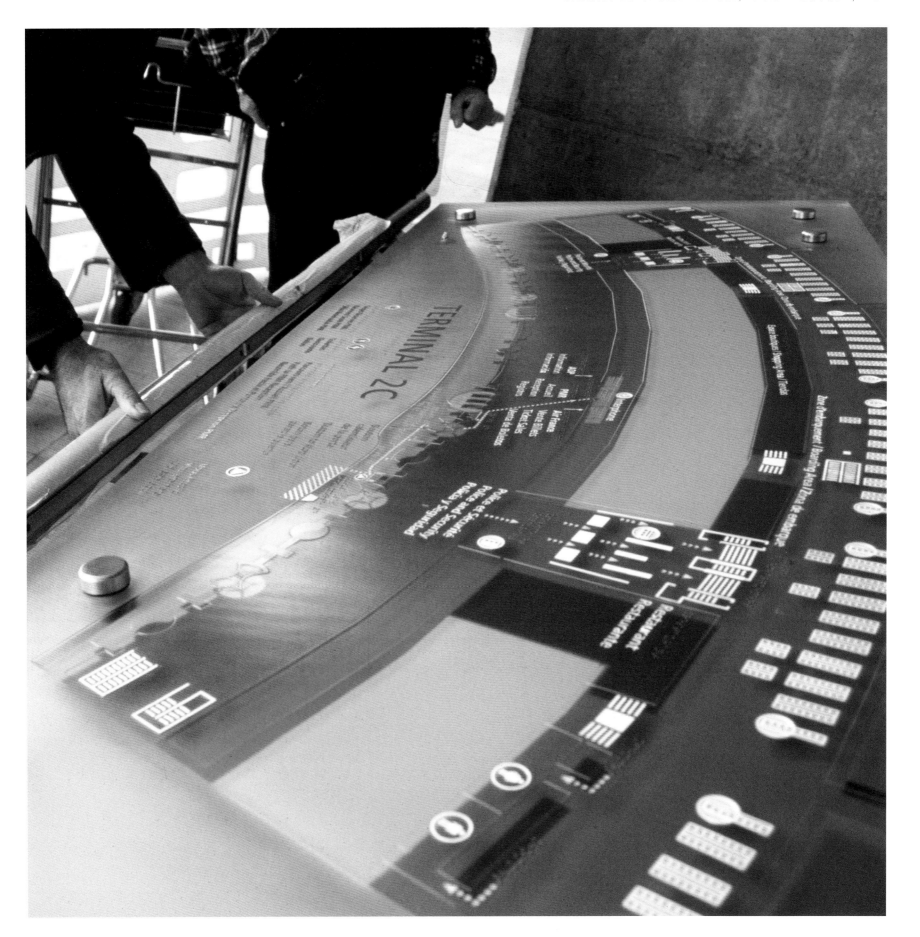

Tacdots, slightly raised dots mounted on the floor, delineate the path already indicated on the tactile map. The dots are bright yellow and make a sound when tapped with a cane. They begin at the sidewalk and ramp drop-off area outside the airport terminal, and lead to the accessible (PMR) reception counter.

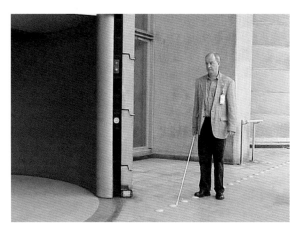

Handrail segments, with Braille
and audio messages activated by
photosensors, are installed at four key
locations along the path. Each rail
presents sequential information and
guides travelers in three languages. The
messages facilitate the navigation of
sight-impared travelers through difficult
areas, such as the revolving door
entrance. The rail segments along the
tactile itinerary are made of galvanized
steel that are powder-coated yellow.

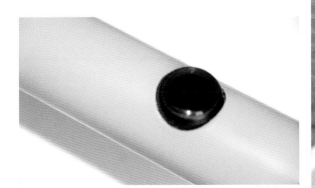

Arab American Hospital
Jeddah, Saudi Arabia

Our design respected the Arabic ornamental tradition with a modern twist.

The interior signage was incorporated into decorative motifs, while the contemporary glass material permitted visual lightness and color contrast.

Details from the façade were simplified to adorn the exterior pylon profiles.

Designers Coco Raynes, Kate Blehar
Architect Steffian Bradley Architects
Completed 2001

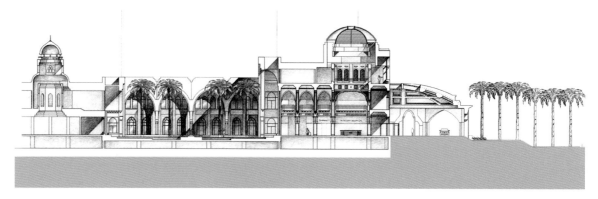

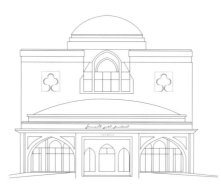

Above: The logo, formed by repeated crescents, alludes to a "tree of life."

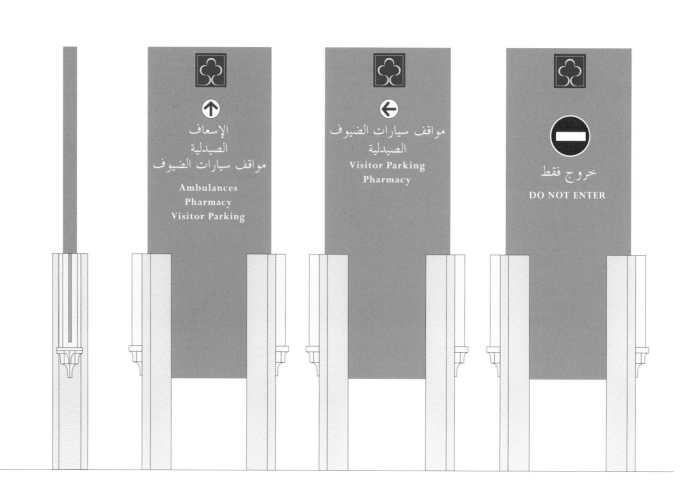

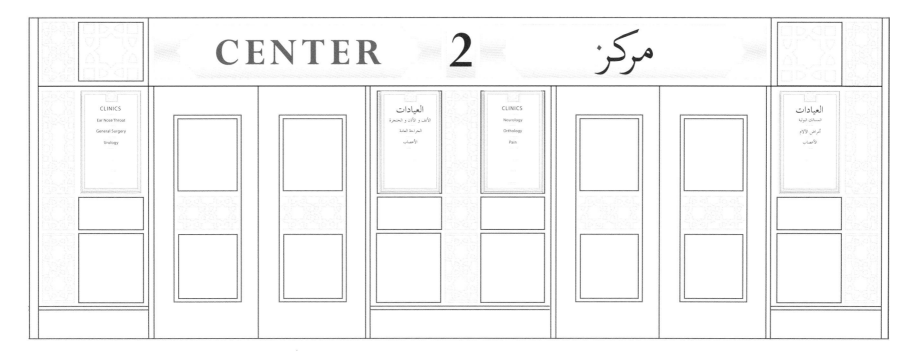

Nurse Station ① وحدة تمريض

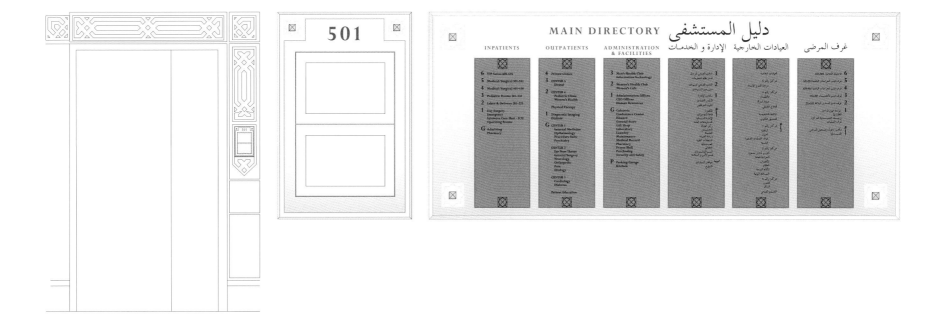

Worcester Public Library
Worcester, Massachusetts
Interior Signage Program

On both floors along the central circulation spine, the columns received the necessary identification and directional information. Glass slabs frame the columns at ninety degrees, allowing messages to be read from different directions.

Designers
Coco Raynes
Kate Blehar

Completed
2003

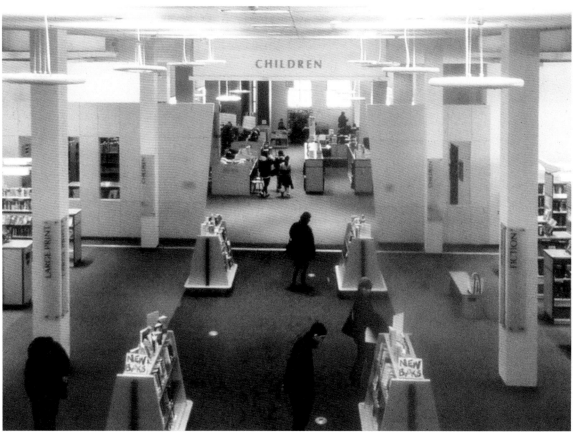

Hebrew College
Newton, Massachusetts

In the middle of the quadrangle, the skylight of the dining room displays the donors' names, which are projected by the sun as shadows along the walls.

Designers Coco Raynes, Kate Blehar

Architect Safdie Architects

Designed 2001

Completed 2003

GOULD

Classical prismatic individual letters identify the buildings.

The glass directory introduces the campus with a clear diagram silhouetted on the frosted surface. The listings are on changeable stainless steel inserts.

One Lincoln
Boston, Massachusetts

Designers
Coco Raynes, Kate Blehar

Client
Gale & Wentworth, LLC

Architect
Jung/Brannen Associates

Completed
2003

ATRIUM

RETAIL STORE NAME

Alternating text

DO NOT ENTER ⊖ CLEARANCE 9.0 FEET ⬆ **EXIT** *LINCOLN ST.*

P1.00a 14'11" x14" Scale: 1/4" = 1'

CLEARANCE 7.0 FEET ENTER ⊕ DO NOT ENTER

P1.00c 14'11" x14" Scale: 1/4" = 1'

On/Off symbol

PUBLIC PARKING ➡

P1.00b 14'11" x14" Scale: 1/4" = 1'

PUBLIC PARKING ➡

P1.00d 14'11" x14" Scale: 1/4" = 1'

Alternating text

⊖ DO NOT ENTER

P1.03a 14'11" x14" Scale: 1/4" = 1'

DO NOT ENTER ⊖ ENTER ⬇ ENTRANCE

P1.02a 14'11" x14" Scale: 1/4" = 1'

On/Off symbol

⬇ ENTRANCE

P1.01a 14'11" x14" Scale: 1/4" = 1'

P1.04a 14'11" x14" Scale: 1/4" = 1'

PUBLIC PARKING ⬅ ➡ ♿ PARKING

P1.05a 14'11" x14" Scale: 1/4" = 1'

PUBLIC PARKING ⬅ ➡ ♿ PARKING

P1.06a 14'11" x14" Scale: 1/4" = 1'

EXIT ⬆ *KINGSTON ST.*

P1.04b 14'11" x14" Scale: 1/4" = 1'

KINGSTON ST. ⬆ **EXIT** ⊖

P1.05b .14'11" x14" Scale: 1/4" = 1'

⊖ DO NOT ENTER

P1.06b 14'11" x14" Scale: 1/4" = 1'

14'11"

All measurements taken from center of sign

3" 9"   26"   26"   9" 3"

14"

DO NOT ENTER ⊖ CLEARANCE 9.0 FEET ⬆ **EXIT** *LINCOLN ST.*

P1.00a 14'11" x14" Scale: 3/4" = 1'

3" 4 1/2" 4 1/2"

PUBLIC PARKING ➡

P1.00b 14'11" x14" Scale: 3/4" = 1'

All measurements taken from center of sign

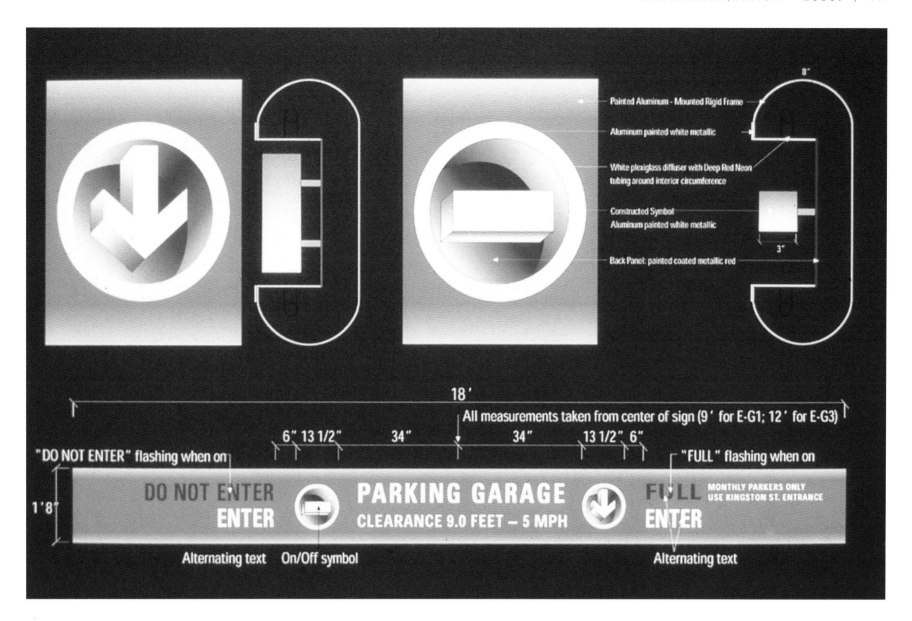

Painted Aluminum - Mounted Rigid Frame

Aluminum painted white metallic

White plexiglass diffuser with Deep Red Neon tubing around interior circumference

Constructed Symbol
Aluminum painted white metallic

Back Panel: painted coated metallic red

18'

All measurements taken from center of sign (9' for E-G1; 12' for E-G3)

6" 13 1/2"   34"   34"   13 1/2" 6"

"DO NOT ENTER" flashing when on

"FULL" flashing when on

1'8"

DO NOT ENTER
ENTER

PARKING GARAGE
CLEARANCE 9.0 FEET – 5 MPH

FULL
ENTER

MONTHLY PARKERS ONLY
USE KINGSTON ST. ENTRANCE

Alternating text   On/Off symbol

Alternating text

DO NOT ENTER

State Street Building
Boston, Massachusetts

State Street leased One Lincoln Street and requested that their name be retrofitted on the tower.

We adapted the existing State Street logo to fit the mullions of the building and created three-dimensional letters, illuminated with neon. The giant sign is seated on the tower as if originally planned.

Designers
Coco Raynes
Kate Blehar

Client
State Street

Architect
Jung/Brannen Associates
Boston, Massachusetts

Completed
2003

Parking Entrance

Further refining the original idea created for 200 Newbury Street, this time the parking symbols were completely integrated into the large beam.

Boston Convention Center
Boston, Massachusetts

The directories are monumental glass slabs with tactile floor plans and listings on changeable stainless steel inserts.

Colors applied to the back surface of the glass further define the maps and link the space to the corresponding listing.

Designers
Coco Raynes
Kate Blehar

Architect
Rafael Viñoly Architects

Completed
2004

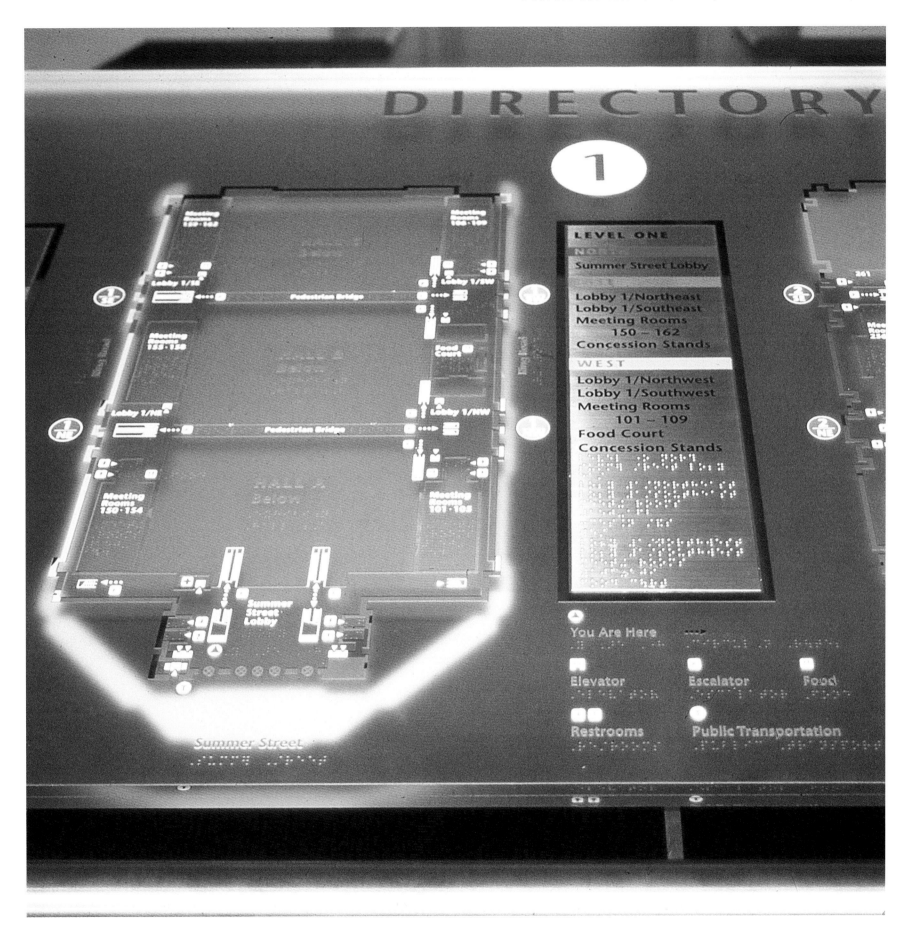

Albert Einstein College of Medicine at Yeshiva University Bronx, New York City

Frosted glass letters were mounted directly on the glass curtain wall.

Architect
Payette, Tom Payette, FAIA

Designers
Coco Raynes, James France

Completed
2007

The monumental granite wall called for old-fashioned hand carving.

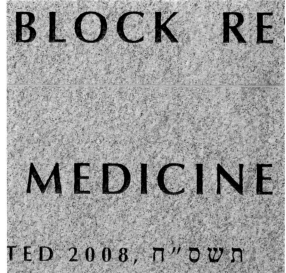

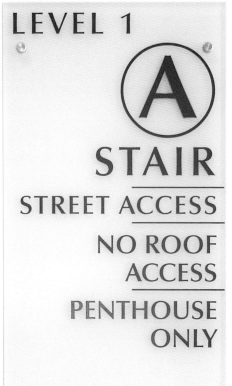

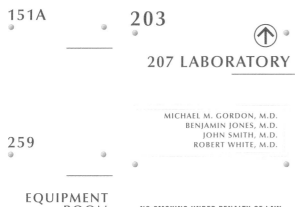

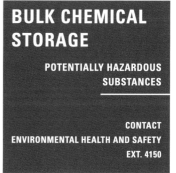

The frosted glass signs complement the sobriety of the interior architecture. They were designed according to a meticulous graphic grid. This same grid was applied to all signs in the building, including to those at back-of-house and laboratory safety regulations signs.

Individual aluminum letters and symbols were used for area naming.

Wall of the Future

Contrasting with the no-frill signage, the Wall of the Future conveys joy and vitality.

Gifts made to the university in the names of donors' children are recognized with individual glass tiles mounted on a glass slab.

In order to control the color harmony, future additions are printed according to the color pattern already established.

Designers Coco Raynes, James France
Completed 2008

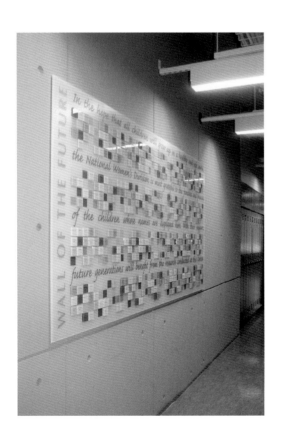

Simmons College
Boston, Massachusetts

On this unique recognition wall, donors for the capital campaign endorsed wise quotes with their name and signature.

Designers Coco Raynes, Kate Blehar

Completed 2008

Battery Park City
Lower Manhattan, New York City

Comprehensive Wayfinding and
Information Program

This program involved our creating a comprehensive information
system that included site surveys, analysis of vehicular and
pedestrian circulation routes, interviews with user-groups,
programming for the signage master plan, conceptual and design
development phases, construction documents, manufacturing
budgets, and a phased implementation plan.

The result was a multisensory wayfinding information system, with
pylons for streets and parks, street signs, kiosks with touch-screens,
and information tables.

Client
Battery Park City Authority
Stephanie Gelb, AIA
Vice President for Planning and Design

Designers
Coco Raynes
Kate Blehar

Completed
2006

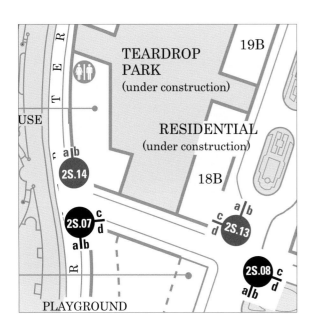

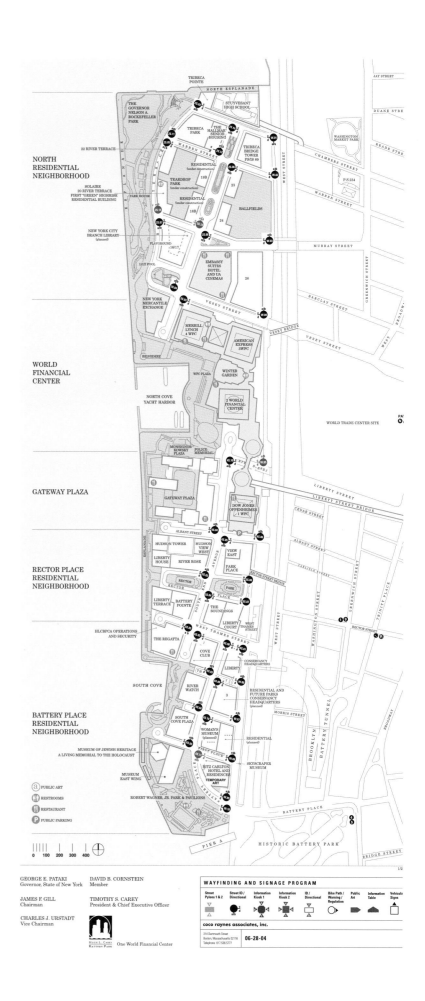

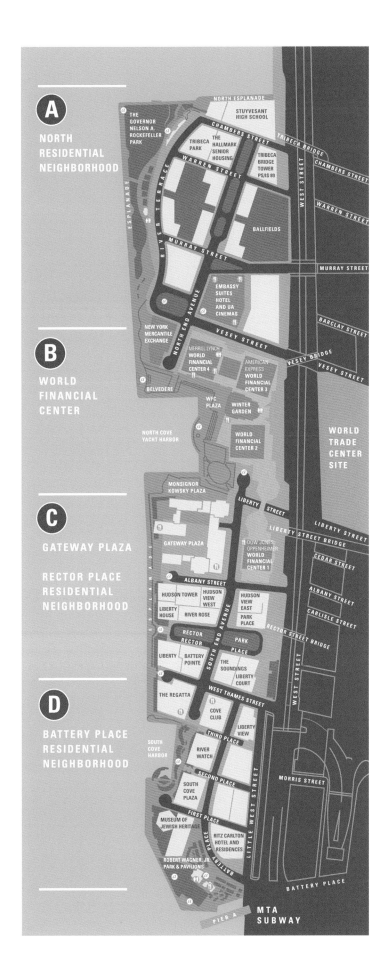

A

NORTH
RESIDENTIAL
NEIGHBORHOOD

B

WORLD
FINANCIAL
CENTER

C

GATEWAY PLAZA

RECTOR PLACE
RESIDENTIAL
NEIGHBORHOOD

D

BATTERY PLACE
RESIDENTIAL
NEIGHBORHOOD

Battery Park City, built entirely
on landfill along the banks of the
Hudson River, is a 6-million-square-
foot area with parks, residential
neighborhoods, schools,
hotels, museums, and retail and
corporate buildings.

The historic site overlooks the
Statue of Liberty and Ellis Island,
and offers one of the country's
most significant and innovative art
programs. Public transportation
includes an MTA Subway station
and bus stops, the Path Commuter
Line, bus shuttles, commuter and
tourist ferries, and water taxis.

Wayfinding and Information System

The multisensory wayfinding and information system introduces the site with tactile maps, raised text, Braille, and audio messages. All glass panels are blasted to present matte surfaces.

The program includes street identification, pylons, kiosks, and slanted information tables.

The pylons, planned for strategic locations along West Street, delineate Battery Park City. They display directional and site information. A stainless steel structure and granite base support the changeable glass panels.

At the South and North entrances of the Park, information tables introduce the New Jersey skyline, Battery Park City, and its public art program—one of the most innovative in the United States.

The accessible sculptures, which can be touched, are identified on the tactile map and described in Braille.

Pylons

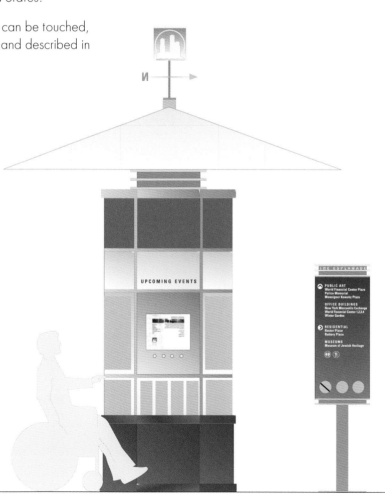

Kiosks

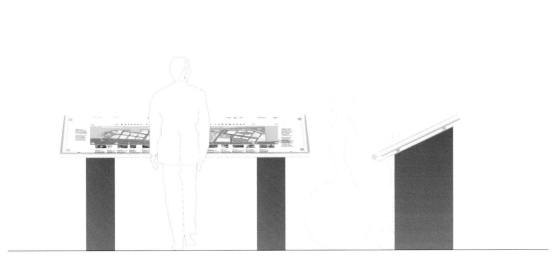

Information tables

Street Identification and Directional Signs

Acrylic with a blasted surface (an unusual material for street signs) was selected not only to create consistency with the overall design vocabulary, but to minimize the intrusion of signage on the site. To address the non-consecutive numbering system, a directional unit lists the buildings by name. We envisioned that the blasted translucent surface would disappear into the sky, giving impact to the text. The two-sided acrylic blades, which are 4 feet long, have been engineered to be non-transparent and hurricane resistant.

A custom-designed attachment ring, made of cast aluminum, permits the heavy signs to be securely mounted to five different kinds of existing lamp posts with varying diameters.

The attachment system accommodates one or two street signs at 90 degrees. A prototype was installed along Rector Place and West Thames Street to test the scale, conditions, and material in the field for two years. The prototype confirms the visual lightness, legibility, and elegance of the acrylic sign, and therefore was approved by the NYC Department of Transporation.

Teardrop Park

Teardrop Park is located within Battery Park City. It offers an exquisite landscaping with a unique planting concept of trees, shrubs, and herbaceous perennials native to the

Hudson Valley Region. The signage for Teardrop Park had to be unobtrusive. With a subtle change of material, the system continues the design vocabulary and philosophy we had already established for Battery Park City.

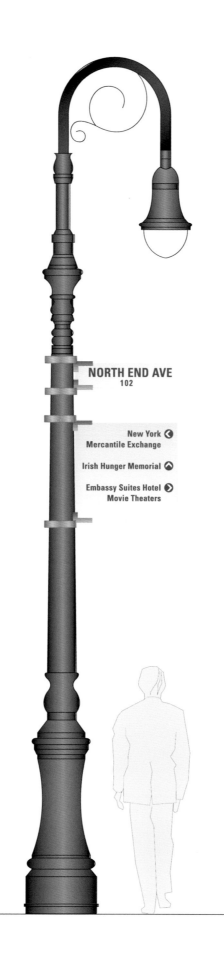

NORTH END AVE
102

New York Mercantile Exchange ◁

Irish Hunger Memorial ◓

Embassy Suites Hotel Movie Theaters ▷

At each of the four Park entrances, a metal pylon displays a tactile map to introduce the planting concept and directs visitors to the exhibits.

Each exhibit presents a detailed raised drawing that highlights the species characteristics, along with large descriptive text and equivalent information in Braille.

The signs are mounted with a simplified version of the attachment ring system designed to secure the street signs.

Marsh
The landform of the Marsh at Teardrop Park collects rainwater from the park, creating a distinctly wet soil condition. A variety of plants suited to wet conditions, ranging from colorful wetland wildflowers to shrubs and trees, grow in this area of the park. The Tupelo tree, also known as Black Gum and Beetle Bung, is a native New England tree that thrives in wet soil. It can be found in low areas in the forests where water collects. The Tupelo tree is highly valued in the landscape for its luminous fall leaf color.

Tupelo Tree *N...sa sylvatica*

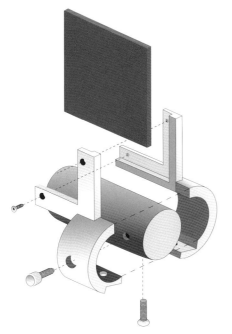

ICE WALL

Do Not Climb

Hebrew SeniorLife
Roslindale, Massachusetts

The multitude of pre-existing donor plaques and other commemorative artifacts were eliminated. We were left with approximately 5,000 donor names to acknowledge, and no wall to display them. The windows received a "glass curtain," with all the names uniformly etched and paint-filled.

Designers Coco Raynes, Kate Blehar
Completed 2006

everyone whose
heart was moved
came, bringing
offerings and
gifts..."

Exodus 35:21

אתו הביאו
את תרומת יהוה
למלאכת אהל
מועד ולכל עבדתו
ולבגדי הקדש

Donor Wall
Elyse and Howard Rubin,
In Honor of Jeremy Robert and
Evan Scott's B'nai Mitzvah

Ark
Marjorie and Alan Tichnor

Sanctuary Design
Karen and Michael Tichnor,
In Honor of Our Children:
Sandra, Ariel, and Samuel

Menorah Sculpture
Sheryl and Marc Schlackman,
In Honor of Ross Brandon's Bar Mitzvah

Elyse and Howard Rubin,
In Honor of Danielle Hope's Bat Mitzvah

Sanctuary Vestibule Floor
Lance Schultz,
In Honor of Ross Brandon's Bar Mitzvah

Piano
Evelyn and John Neumeyer,
Ann Neumeyer and Gary Chinman,
In Memory of Martha Stern Neumeyer
and Irma Stern Midas

Megillah
Karen and Michael Tichnor,
In Honor of Samuel's Bar Mitzvah

In Honor of Our Children and Parents

Elaine and Werner Gossels,
In Honor of Jamie Gossels's Presidency

Social Hall Furniture
Kitah Zayin Class of 2003 / 2004

Bimah Furniture
Kitah Zayin Class of 2004 / 2005

Bench
Kitah Zayin Class of 2005 / 2006

ועשו לי מקדש ושכנתי בתוכם ...AND L

Rabbi
Sally Rena Finestone

Project Management Team
David Fixler   Jonathan Quint
Jamie Gossels   Howard Rubin
Stephen Lebovitz Michael Tichnor

Building Committee Chairpersons
Freya Bernstein   Larry Sternberg
Craig Kaplan   Karen Tichnor
Vicki Kaplan   Stephen Wald
Elyse Rubin   David Winer

Building Committee Members
Gil Fishbein   Sheryl Schlackman
Bonnie Gossels   Amy Silverstein
Jonathan Gossels Marjorie Solomon
Deborah Horwitz   Millie Tubman
Barry Katz   Barbara Winer
Debbie Mikels   James Wolfson
Warren Morss

Groundbreaking
September 16, 2001; 28 Elul 5761

Torah Procession
September 1, 2002; 24 Elul 5762

Building Dedication
March 8, 2003; 4 Adar II 5763

Bimah Dedication
December 11, 2004; 28 Kislev 5765

Architect
Bruner / Cott & Associates, Inc.
Construction Firm
Elaine Construction Company, Inc.

Sanctuary Pews
Joel Wald,
In Memory of Muriel Wald

Janet and Sidney Quint,
In Honor of Judy and Jonathan Quint's
20th Wedding Anniversary

Suzanne and Richard Wiesman,
In Honor of Joshua, David, and
Ben Wiesman

Marilyn and Joshua Engelman
and Irene Fishman,
In Loving Memory of
Donald Fishman

Alice and Murray Goldstein,
In Honor of Our Children
and Grandchildren:
Vicki, Craig, Bill and Shari Kaplan

Vivienne Kalman,
In Honor of Ross and Amy Silverstein

Jamie and Jon Gossels and
Larry and Nancy Rowe,
In Honor of Our Parents:
Benson and Marcia Rowe

Jerome Sternberg,
In Honor of Larry Sternberg
and Sara Abramovitz

Congregation Or Atid,
In Honor of Jamie Gossels's Presidency

Barbara and David Winer,
In Honor of Our Children:
Jesse, Lee, and Jenna

Congregation Or Atid,
In Honor of Larry Sternberg's Presidency

Congregation Or Atid,
In Honor of David Winer
For His Many Years
Of Service to the Synagogue

The Board of Directors,
Congregation Or Atid,
In Honor of Judy Quint's Presidency

Congregation Or Atid,
In Honor of the 25th Anniversary of
Rabbi Finestone's Ordination

Harriet and Paul Rosen,
In Memory of Our Parents:
Celia and David Rosen,
and Claire and Max Strauss

Barbara and David Winer,
In Honor of Congregation Or Atid's
Founding Families

Congregation Or Atid
Wayland, Massachusetts

Designers Coco Raynes, Kate Blehar
Completed 2006

Again, all donors are honored
together on one single glass
recognition wall, which adorns
the empty corridor.

The names are engraved
in white against three distinctive
color backgrounds, applied
to the back surface.

A bronze beam provides
visual interest and helps
support the heavy panels.

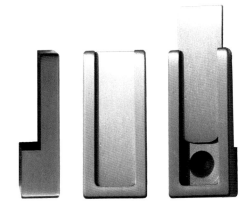

Beth Sholom Synagogue
Memphis, Tennessee

Murals are etched on glass panels with Psalms 146, 147, 148, 149, and 150.

The sacred texts form a cloud on the glass, alluding to a prayer in the sky.

Designers Coco Raynes, Kate Blehar

Architect Finegold Alexander Architects
Maurice Finegold, FAIA

Completed 2001

Photography: Charles Davis Smith, FAIA

**Congregation Shearith Israel
Dallas, Texas**

Architect Finegold Alexander Architects, Maurice Finegold, FAIA

Designers Coco Raynes, James France

Completed 2007

Miriam Hospital
Providence, Rhode Island
Building Identification Sign

The retrofitted sign blends seamlessly
with the architecture of the building.

Designers
Coco Raynes
James France

Completed
2006

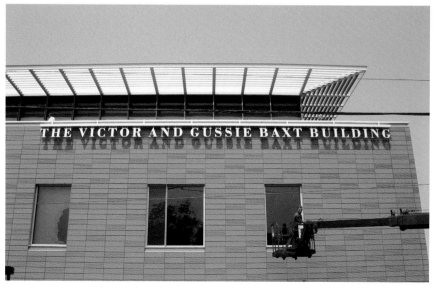

Four Seasons Hotel at Park Square
Boston, Massachusetts
Exhibit Kiosk

The kiosk, which camouflages a
ventilation shaft of the nearby Four
Season Hotel, was also an opportunity
to engage residents and visitors in
the history of the city. On one side,
a large map depicts at a glance
the landfill of Back Bay, which was
once underwater. The other side
introduces the development of the
Boston Providence Railroad, a colossal
construction endeavor at the time.
Detailed photographs and engravings
further illustrate the historical evolution
of the area, from 1630 to the present.

The graphics are etched and paint-
filled on black-coated stainless steel.
The seams of the panels are minimized
by the graphic layout.

Architect
CBT Architects
Richard Bertman, FAIA
Eric Vogel

Designers
Coco Raynes
Kate Blehar

Completed
2006

Worcester Trial Court
Worcester, Massachusetts
Interior and Exterior Signage Program

A very classical approach was appropriate for this public edifice. Individual bronze color letters and seals complement the austere wooden paneling.

The scale of the courtroom identification avoided unnecessary directional signs: all the entrances can be read directly from the elevator landing.

Designers Coco Raynes, Kate Blehar

Architect Shepley Bulfinch

Completed 2007

Fall River Justice Center
Fall River, Massachusetts
Interior and Exterior Signage Program

The signage respected the palette of the interior finishes, using either blasted glass surfaces or matte beige photopolymer. The directory maps are tactile, and the aluminum inserts can easily be changed to accommodate new listings.

Designers
Coco Raynes
James France

Architect
Finegold Alexander Architects
Maurice Finegold, FAIA

Completed
2008

Tufts University
School of Dental Medicine
Boston, Massachusetts
Comprehensive Wayfinding and
Donor Recognition Program

Monumental white letters trimmed in
aluminum identify the building, recalling
the reveal detail of the façade tiles.
Instead of the standard Tufts University
Blue, the monochromatic palette sets
the white tower apart from its crowded
surroundings.

Designers
Coco Raynes
James France

Completed
2009

To enhance the elegance and luminosity of the glass curtain along the main corridors, door signs and donor recognition plaques were eliminated.

The glass panels by the doors were blasted entirely to become the signs: large graphics identify the departments, laboratories, and offices; tactile letters and Braille are positioned according to ADA and state regulations to meet the code requirements.

Glass signs were designed for the secondary corridors; some with a hinge attachment to float in front of the windows.

THIS SUITE
MADE POSSIBLE
BY A GIFT FROM
DR. LOUIS A. FIORE D62,
AND MRS. JEAN H. FIORE

Above: Eliminating the need for plaques, the donor names are incorporated into the sidelight panels, engraved and paint-filled on-site below the Tufts University seal.

...ARD M. CARNEY, JR., A31, D34
GERALD R. CARRIER, D60
REGINALD J. CARROLL, D47
WALTER A. CARUSO, D52
DONALD W. CASSIDY, D60, D88P
SANTO S. CATAUDELLA, D55, J88P
ROBERT J. CELLA, A49, D51, D76P
HAROLD A. CHAMBERLIN, JR., D53
CHAYES DENTAL INSTRUMENT CORPORATION
LEVON CHERTAVIAN, D50
ELMER H. CHESTER, D40
CHARLES G. CHIGAS, A40, D44

...SUPPLY COMPANY
DENTSPLY INTERNATIONAL, INC.
DONALD L. DESCHENES, D54
ROBERT A. DESROCHERS, D61
NORMAN H. DIAMOND, D57, DG64, A30P
RALPH B. DIAMOND, D35
RICHARD J. DICK, D54
GARY C. DICKERMAN, A52, D56
GEORGE B. DINAN, D48
MARTIN J. DIONNE, D53
JOSEPH J. DIPIETRO, D54, D81P, A86P, D87P
FRANK A. DIPIRO, D59, A87P, J92P
EUGENE R. DISTASIO, A52, D57, DG66
HENRY J. DIVAIO, D46
H. CHRIS DOKU, D58, DG60, J84P

...DG51, A75P, D78P, DG83P
NORMAN E. FULLER, D56
ANTHONY P. GAIESKI, D43
RALPH W. GALEN, D52
JAMES B. GALLAGHER, JR., A47, D49, DG68
JOHN F. GALLAGHER, JR., A45, D51
IRVING H. GARBER, D52
DR. CYRIL GAUM
ROSS I.V. GELDART, D56, DG58
MORRIS GELLER, D42
THE GENERAL FOOD FUND, INC.
EDWARD L. GERSTEIN, D55
DR. DONALD B. GIDOON
PHILIP E. GIGUERE, D59
MR. AND MRS. CARL J. GILBERT
GEORGE T. GILDEA, D52, DG53
NEVILLE D. GILMORE, D50, DG58, DG60

...NALD M. HEATON, D15
RICHARD M. HEILIGMANN, D34
HENRY J. HEIM, D56
RUSSEL HENRIKSEN, A52, D56
JOHN L. HICKEY, D39
LOUIS HIMMELFARB, D54
DR. SUMNER HIRSHBERG
MILTON HODOSH, D54, D79P, D87P
EVERETT M. HOFFMAN, D44
RICHARD F. HOOD, D57
HAROLD L. HORTON, D60, DG64
ROBERT E. HOWARD, D58
MR. AND MRS. WESTON HOWLAND, JR., H96
HOWMET CORPORATION
HU-FRIEDY MANUFACTURING COMPANY INC.
MELVIN L. HUTNER, D44, DG52, DG53, J84P, D86P
KENNETH R. HYDE, D46
ABRAHAM E. HYMAN, D29
JOHN C. IRONS, JR., D14
RODERICK W. LEWIN, D51

HEARTFELT GRATITUDE TO THE VISIONARY MEN AND WOMEN WHO OFFERED PHILANTHR...

APRIL

BUILDING

WILLIAM G. CHIGAS, A55, D59, A80P, A82P
ROBERT E. CHODROFF, D65, J89P
ARTHUR G. CIAMPA, D59, J94P
ACHILLE J. CIARAMELLO, D48
CARL L. CLAPP, D62
GEORGE H. CLARKE, A35, D37
D. EDWARD CLEARY, A43, D44
MARY AND HARRY COAN, D28
COE LABORATORIES
ANTHONY C. COGLIANO, D35
M. MICHAEL COHEN, D28
MITCHELL M. COHEN, D40
ESTHER, D42 AND RALPH COLCHAMIRO
RAYMOND F. COLE, JR., D45
DOMENIC A. CONCA, D48
JOSEPH B. CONNOLLY, DB43, D76P
JOHN J. CONNOR, D55, E88P
ANGELO R. CONTARINO, D47
DAVID M. COOLEY, D46
SAMUEL M. COPE, D38
FRANCIS R. COPPOLA, A29, D33
JOSEPH V. CORRIVEAU, D46
WILLIAM A. CORRIVEAU, A48, D51
ROBERT E. CORVI, D64
JOHN S. COUGHLAN, D47
...COUGHLIN, D44

O. WALTER DONNENFELD, DG54
RICHARD J. DOWD, D58
JOHN D. DOYKOS III, A59, D62, DG65, A09P, J94P
NATHAN L. DUBIN, D34
ROBERT B. DUHAIME, D61
MAURICE H. DUMAS, D33
L. NORMAN DUTTON, D51
JOSEPH M. DWORKIN, D53, D81P
THE EASTERN ASSOCIATED FOUNDATION
NATHAN EDELBERG, D34
RAYMOND H. EGER, D60
FRANK A. EICH, A42, D44
ERWIN M. ELDRIDGE, D55
GORDON B. EMONT, D54
ROBERT H. ENDERSON, D60
ARTHUR R. FALVEY, JR., D60, J84P
ARMAND R. FAMIGLIETTI, D33
GEORGE J. FANNING, D48
ANDREW J. FARQUHAR, A31, D35
NORMAN H. FARR, JR., D53
GEORGE A. FAULKNER, JR., D47
SAMUEL J. FEARING, D53
SAMUEL B. FELDMAN, D30
EDWIN S. FIELDS III, D61
ROBERT S. FIELDS, D54, DG59, J85P
JOHN J. FINN, A53, D56

RICHARD C. GINGRAS, D50
ANNA GINTOWT, D55
CALVIN V. GIUSTI, D52
SAMUEL I. GLASER, A23, D27
SIDNEY B. GLASSMAN, D57, DG59
CHARLES A. GLEASON, D29
IRVING GLICKMAN, D38
C. JOEL GLOVSKY, A54, D57, DG61, A80P, D83P, DG85P
ARTHUR GOLD, DG47
THEODORE F. GOLDBERG, D39
LEO GOLDEN, D28
MELVIN GOLDMAN, D.D.S.
GORDON G. GOMBAR, D58
DAVID S. GORDON, D40
JEROME GORDON, D53
RODERICK M. GOYETTE, D61
WILLIAM G. GRAHAM, D57, DG59
DR. DAVID GRAINGER
ROBERT S. GRAY, D45
DR. ORRIN GREENBERG
ROBERT P. GRIFFIN, D54
ALAN J. GROVER, D53
ALLEN GRUNIN, A44, D47
HARRY H. GULESIAN, A37, D39
FLOYD B. GULICK, D34
MR. AND MRS. WILLIAM J. HALLIGAN
DR. AND MRS. BURTON C. HALLOWELL, H76

J.F. JELENKO COMPANY, INC.
ROBERT F. JACKSON, D56
FORREST A. JACOBS, A45, D46
DION S. JANETOS, D41
JEWEL FOUNDATION
LEIF B. JOHANNESSEN, D49
ERLING JOHANSEN, D49
DR. RUDOLPH B. JOHNSON
LEONARD R. JOHNSTON, D31
JOHN A. KACEWICZ, D58, DG52
JOHN F. KAIN, A43, D44
JOEL A. KALAFA, DG64
DR. SAMUEL KANE
MILTIADES KARAMECHEDIS, D60
JOEL R. KARP, D59
THADDEUS J. KARWACKI, D43
FRANK D. KASPARIAN, A58, D61, J91P, J92P, D17P, DG51P
GERARD KASS, D58, DG62
HOWARD M. KASSLER, A51, D55
ALBERT J. KAZIS, D43, J70P
FREDERICK P. KEACH, D45
JOHN F. KELLER, A44, D45
DONALD F. KEMNITZER, D53
GEORGE A. KEMPSTER, D37
HENRY KENT, D62
WILLIAM E. KIDDER, D47
M. LEO KIERNAN

A. BUDNER LEWIS, D33
CLYDE C. LEWIS, D56
MR. AND MRS. JACOB LEWITON, A30, J75P
ROLAND A. L'HEUREUX, D58
HOWARD R. LIBBY, D41
RAYMOND S. LICHT, D48, DG54
MATHEW A. LIPSKY, D47, DG51
STANLEY E. LISTERNICK, A50, D55, AG51
ROBERT J. LITWIN, D51
LASZLO J. LORINCZ, D57, M79P, D85P
DR. RONALD E.R. LOVELL
PHILIP W. LOWN
JOHN D. LUCAS, D55, DG59
GORDON G. MACALASTER, D44
WILLIAM D. MACINTOSH, D24
JOHN A. MACLAUGHLIN, D52
DONALD C. MACLEOD, A54, D56
MRS. ELMORE I. MACPHIE
DWIGHT R. MAGOVERN, A56, D57
GARY D. MAILANDER, D63, DG64
GEORGE A. MAILLARD, A50, D54
HENRY C. MALGODDI, JR., D56
PHILIP L. MALONEY, D55, AG92P...
STUART J. MANCHESTER, D50
AGISILAOS P. MANICKAS, D57, DG74, J86P, D91P
JAMES C. O'DONNELL, D58, DG62

CARL J. MONACELLI, D41
BENSON MONASTERSKY, D64, DG68, A35P, J91P
DALE B. MONTGOMERY, D18
MR. AND MRS. DANIEL J. MONTGOMERY
RICHARD MOORADKANIAN, D61
EDWARD MARSHALL MORIN, DG52
ROBERT S. MORRIS, A50, D56, J68P
GERALDINE T. MORROW, D50, H92
IRENE K. MOTSWILLERS, D59
GARRY T. MOUSHEGIAN, D58
ROBERT D. MOYNIHAN, A54, D56
JOHN W. MUGAR, H37
PAUL T.P. MURPHY, A54, D57
RONALD E. MYERS, D58
EDWARD S. NAHIGIAN, A36, D42
W. LAWRENCE NANKEN, JR., D58
DR. NORMAN NATHANSON
THE NATIONAL SHAWMUT BANK
JAMES NASMYK, A36, D58
EVANS H. NELSON, D18
MORTON NETUPSKY, D48, J90P
NEW ENGLAND REGIONAL COMMISSION
THE J.M. NEY COMPANY
RICHARD E. NICKERSON, D58
ERNEST E. NUFER, JR., D58
OBRION, RUSSELL & COMPANY

WILLIAM T. PIKE, D40
WILLIAM J. PINGREE, D44, DG66, J88P
PETER E. POOL, D61
ROGER A. PRESTON, D41
JOSEPH C. PRIMACK, A48, D42, A36P, M39P, A30P
FREDERICK PROSE, JR., D16
PAUL G. PROVOST, D52
BARRY PUCKROFF, D56
PULPDENT CORP. OF AMERICA
JAMES E. RAHAL, D29
ANTHONY J. RAMOS, D50
HAROLD R. KATCHOROS, D50
JOHN G. REICHELLE, D52
MR. AND MRS. JOEL M. REYNOLDS
EUGENE E. RHEAULT, D42
MURRAY A. RICE, D46
OLIVE I. RICE
CLIFFORD E. RICHARDS, D16
HENRY R. RICHARDSON, D44
BARNARD H. RICKER, D44, D43

Donor Recognition

The Donor Wall continue the transparent and luminous vocabulary started with the signage. The various generations of plaques installed since the early 70s were dismounted and inventoried.

Present and past donor names were assembled on the new wall, along a giant time line. In the back ground is an inspirational quote from Winston Churchill.

Consistent with the format of the department identification, exceptionally large gifts are acknowledged with a full size portrait of either the donor or the person being honored along with a personal message.

The Modern Theatre,
Suffolk University
Boston, Massachusetts
Marquis and Interior Signage Program

Located in the Boston theater district, the Suffolk University theater needed presence, but with academic restraint.

Therefore the marquee does not scream for attention and respects the proportions of this historic façade.

The interior signs combine brown glass plaques with a cast bronze leaf attachment inspired from original building details.

Designers
Coco Raynes, James France

Architect
CBT Architects, Richard Bertman, FAIA

Completed
2008

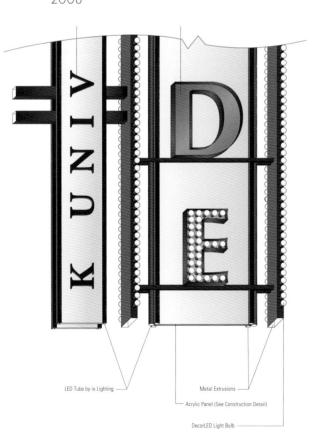

LED Tube by io Lighting

Metal Extrusions

Acrylic Panel (See Construction Detail)

DecorLED Light Bulb

W Boston
Interior and Exterior Signage

The hotel is located in a high-traffic area, and the signs needed to stand out. A neon technique was selected for the hotel name, and deep, three-dimensional aluminum letters were designed for the entrance.

Internally illuminated individual letters designate the main areas.

The unusual hotel guest room sign receives the morning newspaper.

Photography: courtesy William Rawn Associates, Architects, Inc./TRO Jung Brannen Inc.

Client Sawyer Enterprises, Inc.

Designer Coco Raynes

Completed 2009

Design
Coco Raynes
Kate Blehar

Leaf Casting
Danielle Bessudo

Designed
2005-2006

As a diversion from the serious work of wayfinding and accessibility, one day we decided to be light-hearted, perhaps even frivolous, and create a jewelry collection. We applied our experience in industrial and signage design; it was the same approach—only the scale had changed.

Immediately we dove into the work, fearlessly using valuable pearls mixed with unusual elements. It became the office tradition twice a year: we would transform the space into a jewelry gallery for an elegant opening. When we stopped—because we could no longer keep up the pace—our clients complained!

**Black Coral, Onyx,
and Pearl Necklace**

Designer Coco Raynes
Designed 2006

The pendants are removable and interchangeable—as a normal modular system—with tiny screws inserted into the pearls.

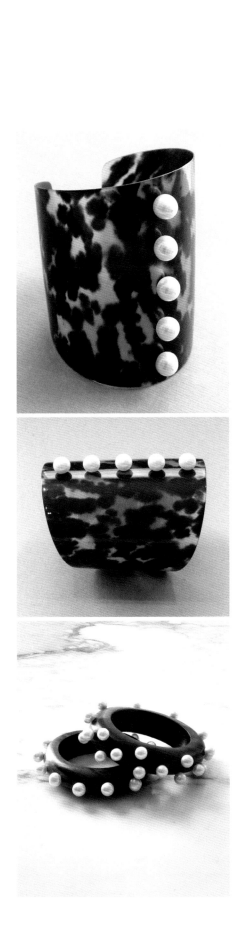

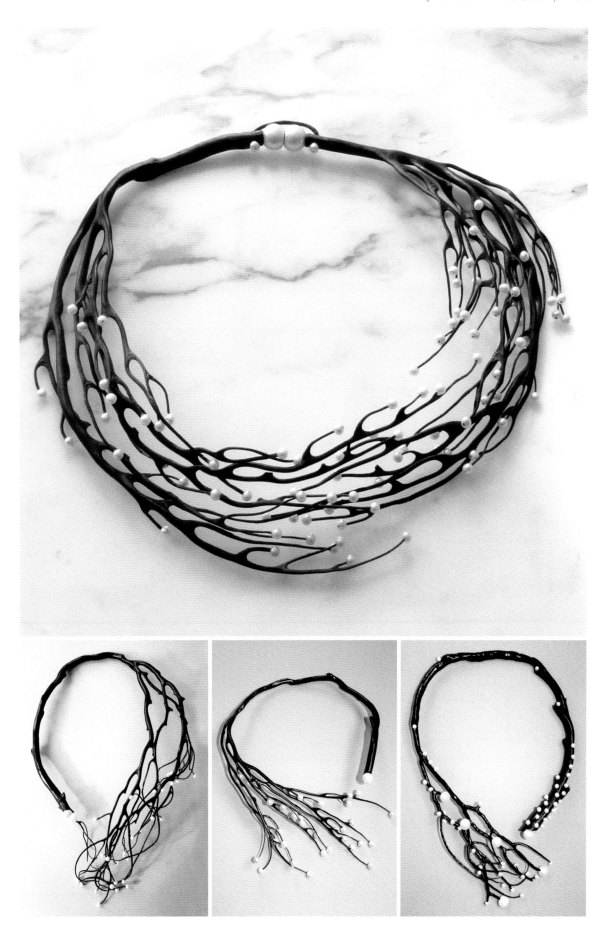

Supporting the Jimmy Fund was important, and we made time to participate in the international public art exhibit that is the Boston CowParade.

Boston CowParade
benefitting The Jimmy Fund

Bilingual Cow

Sponsored by The French Library and Cultural Center Alliance Française of Boston

This is truly a modern cow—bilingual, at ease in the world, mixing a certain elegance with a relaxed outfit of leggings, bustier, formal pearls and high heels, fit for a summer's day in the city.

Her dressing is made of poppies, daisies, and bluets—the "fleurs des champs" of France. The carpet she stands on is an allusion to the Tapisseries aux Milles Fleurs.

Her pearl necklace is accented with a red ruby. A photosensor-activated audio message introducing the summer program of the French Library is in both French and English—and sings "La Vie en Rose."

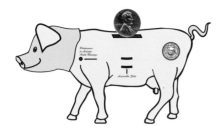

Piggy Bank Cow

Sponsored by the Cambridge Trust Company, Inc.

The cow was disguised as a piggy bank, adorned with a giant penny in the money slot. The photosensor-activated audio messages recite wisdom quotes from famous authors.

Above: The conference room was temporarily occupied by the cows while they waited to make their debut on the streets of Boston.

Designers
Coco Raynes, Kate Blehar

Fabrication Team
Coco Raynes Associates, Inc.
Design Communications, Ltd.
Nabil Lamriben

Completed
2006

William D. Smith Memorial Award for Preservation and Accessibility 2013
Massachusetts Architectural Access Board

Achievement Award 2013
Boston Preservation Alliance

Silver Award 2012 (two nominations)
International Design

BSA Design Award 2011
Boston Society of Architects

2010s

By now, the office has been recognized for its design innovation. The scale of projects and their nature have evolved significantly; we are designing comprehensive wayfinding programs for very large sites.

Regardless of the program size and complexity, however, the rules have not changed. Wherever the project is, the design must blend with the surroundings, reflect the local culture, and be accessible to all.

My creative design process is still triggered by the need to solve a problem. It starts with conversations with the client and design team, accompanied by an in-depth understanding of the project and assessment of possible opportunities. Then, the interplay between existing data and creative intuition merges to become an original design.

Aga Khan University, Faculty of Arts & Sciences Karachi, Pakistan

Comprehensive information system for a 500-acre site, with multiple buildings woven around courtyards.

Phase I of construction consisted of 26 buildings exceeding 2.5 million square feet of residential, teaching, and athletics facilities.

Wayfinding System Based on a Numeric Address

We designed a numeric address system based on the triaxial organization of the campus, allowing for future growth. It reflects a hierarchy of information: numbers for primary axis, building, level, and room.

Architect
Payette
Tom Payette, FAIA
Mark Careaga, AIA

Designers
Coco Raynes
James France

Completed
2011

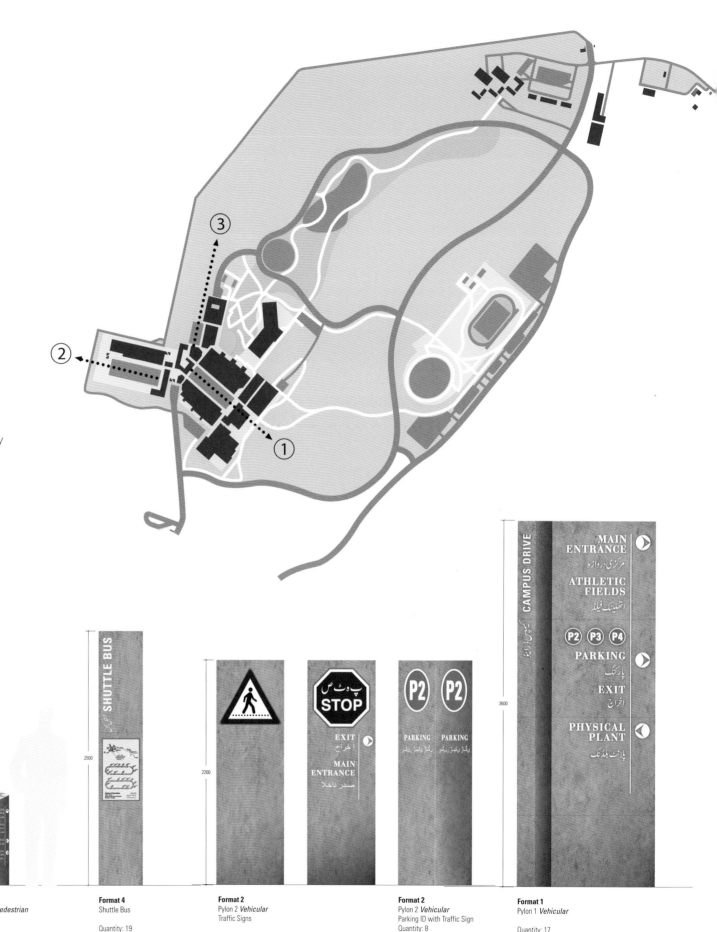

Format 3
Trail Marker *Pedestrian*

Quantity: 22

Format 4
Shuttle Bus

Quantity: 19

Format 2
Pylon 2 *Vehicular*
Traffic Signs

Format 2
Pylon 2 *Vehicular*
Parking ID with Traffic Sign
Quantity: 8

Format 1
Pylon 1 *Vehicular*

Quantity: 17

Information and Directional Signs

The modular information system—made of changeable porcelain tiles—was designed on a single-tile format that reflects the grid established by the Indian National Standard brick. The typography and diagrams are etched and paint-filled on the tiles, recalling the traditional local art of stone carving.

The three axes of growth—academic, arts, and graduate—serve as the primary level of orientation.

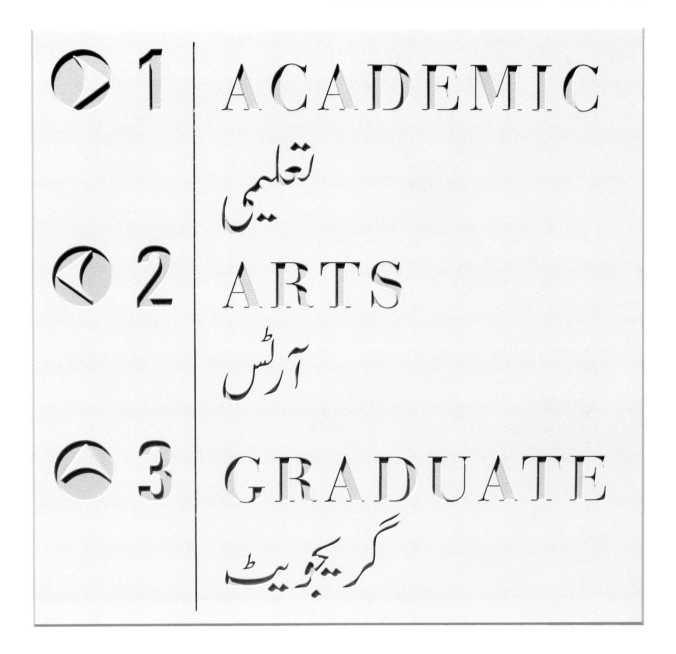

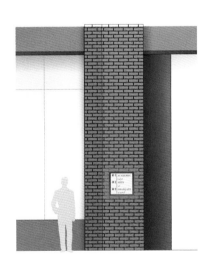

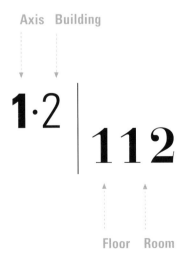

Axis Building

1·2

112

Floor Room

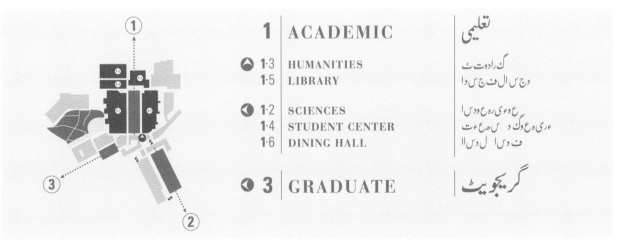

Orientation Diagrams and Modular Tile System

The orientation diagrams are based on the same system of deeply engraved porcelain tiles. The map rotates based on the position of the viewer.

The axes are presented graphically without words. They establish a visual language that eliminates the need for translation.

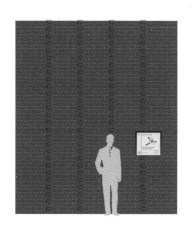

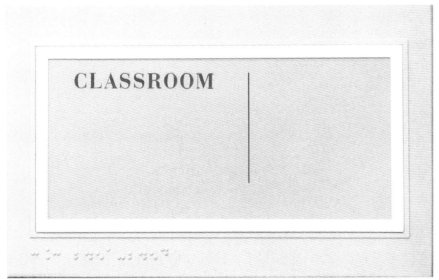

Door Identification

The dual-door sign system is designed for 90-degree installation, and made of etched porcelain with an acrylic insert.

We had been instructed to work according to the ADA codes, which meant that the door signs would be positioned by the doors. For a blind visitor it would also mean going in and out of each door alcove, until the desired room was found (Diagram A).

Instead, we elected to work according to common sense: the permanent information is displayed consistently along the corridor (Diagram B), while the changeable schedules are displayed within the recessed door areas.

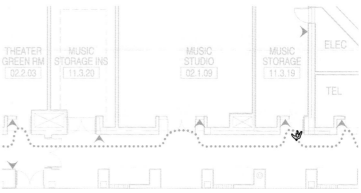

Diagram A

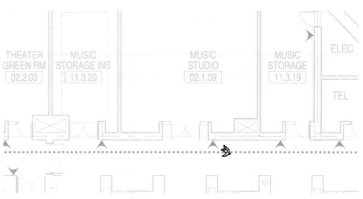

Diagram B

NewBridge on the Charles
Dedham, Massachusetts

Comprehensive Wayfinding, Signage and Donor Recognition Program

NewBridge on the Charles is a multi-generation campus with twenty buildings, including residences, a community center, healthcare facilities, assisted living, and memory support.

Designers

Coco Raynes, Kate Blehar, James France

Completed

2009

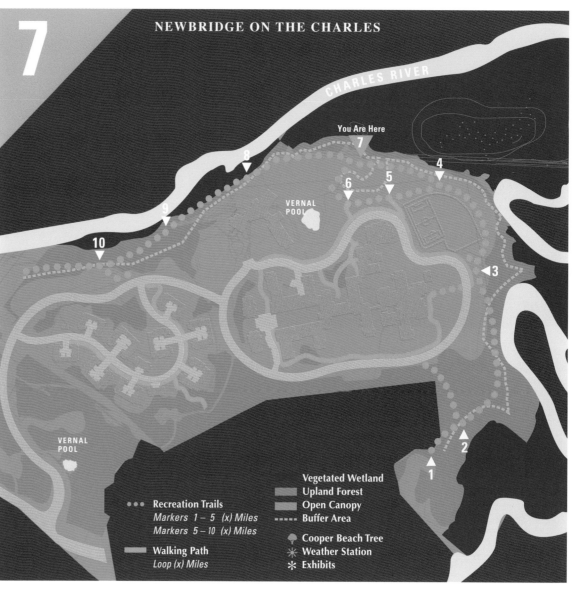

We wanted the signs on the grounds to blend with the architecture and landscape design, therefore we created stone walls for the sole purpose of acknowledging donors prominently.

Exterior Signs

The design and colors are reminiscent of the buildings' architectural details, and established the vocabulary for the exterior wayfinding program.

Directional signs are easily changeable in view of future additions. They are inserted into interlocking structures of smaller scale. Traffic regulations are incorporated into the system.

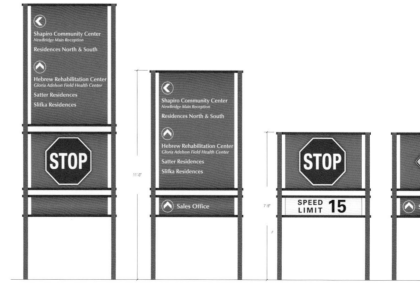

Kotler Community Garden Entrance Gateway

A rustic version of a gateway was unanimously approved in place of the recognition plaque that had been planned for the tool shed.

Cafeteria and Bakery

NewBridge on the Charles offers several
dining venues. The identities of the cafeteria
and coffee shop contrast with the formality of
the other restaurants.

Photography: courtesy Wikimedia Commons/Editorpana

Biomuseo
Panama City, Panama
Emergency Signage

The museum design team had forgotten to include basic information and emergency signs, without which the museum could not open. We were asked to design and coordinate the manufacturing of the program in less than ten days. We happily complied, with etched and tactile aluminum signs.

Designer
Coco Raynes

Completed
2014

EXTINTOR

ALARMA MANUAL

CONEXIÓN PARA MANGUERA

SALIDA DE EMERGENCIA CON ALARMA

Boston Architectural College
Boston, Massachusetts
Identification Sign
on Historic Building

The sign-balancing act was dictated
by the constrictions imposed on us: no
drilling on the stones of this historic
building, and as few drilling holes as
possible in the mortar.

The hollow aluminum letters are
inserted on the cast acrylic support.
They house the lighting that makes the
frosted surface glow.

Designer
Coco Raynes

Completed
2012

Baystate Medical Center
Springfield, Massachusetts
Donor Recognition

This majestic wall is designed to be read in three sequences: first, the inspirational message to be viewed as one enters the very large lobby; then the appreciation text from the institution to the donors; and finally the donors' names.

The aluminum tracks support the glass panels and the individual metal letters, and house the lighting.

The modular glass panels are composed of two layers: the back layer has deep carved letters and color on the back surface, while the front layer presents the engraved donor names. Two new plaques are added each year.

Client
Baystate Health Foundation

Architect
Steffian Bradley Architects
Peter Steffian, FAIA

Designers
Coco Raynes
Kate Blehar

Completed
2012

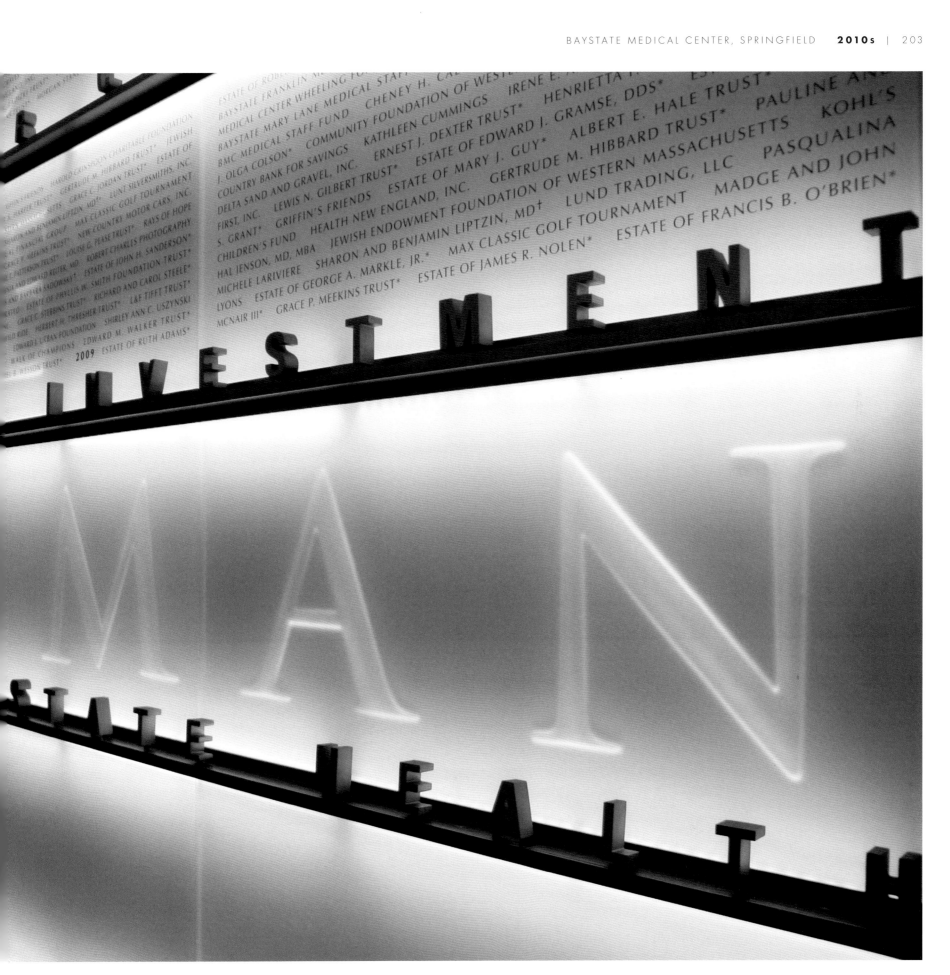

Baystate Medical Center
Springfield, Massachusetts
Donor Recognition

For this specific donor recognition wall, we selected contrasting materials—black and sienna glass against pale limestone, formally carved with V-cut letters.

Designers Coco Raynes

Client Baystate Health Foundation

Completed 2012

Sofitel Legend Santa Clara
Cartagena, Colombia
Interior Signage Program

Built in 1621, this convent is now a five-star hotel. Signs had to be discreet, elegant, and blend with the Spanish Colonial architecture. Once more we elected to design a unique bronze attachment. The upper part of the hotel logo is made of bronze; the lower half is raised on the etched glass surface, creating the illusion of reflection.

Designers Coco Raynes, James France

Client Sofitel Luxury Hotels, AccorHotels

Completed 2012

Blue Glass Cafe
Boston, Massachusetts
Terrace Design and
Exterior Signage

Blue Glass Cafe was hidden behind the dark glass of the Boston John Hancock Tower. When asked to advertise the café with a pylon, we responded with the design of an entire outdoor terrace, which brought a new vitality to the street and substantially increased the restaurant's visibility and seating capacity.

To address the location in the windiest corridor of the city, custom-designed tables hide heavy umbrella bases, each with an individual weight equivalent to that of a small car.

Designers
Coco Raynes
Stephanie Mallis, FAIA

Client
The Blue Glass Cafe

Completed
2013

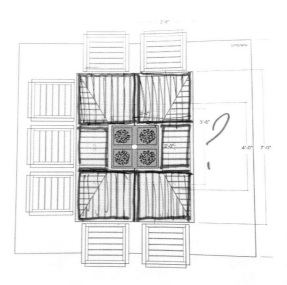

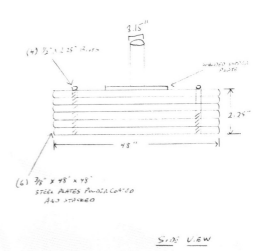

Cinestudio, Trinity College
Hartford, Connecticut
Sign Design

A Trinity College alumnus had seen the Boston Architectural College sign and wanted to donate exactly the same one to Cinestudio, which was not possible, of course.

Located on the college campus, the building's small façade is visible from the street, but from a great distance it's obscured.

Cinestudio's new sign and lighting welcomes the public and can change color for special events.

Shown below are the other design options presented.

Designer Coco Raynes

Client Cinestudio

Designed 2016

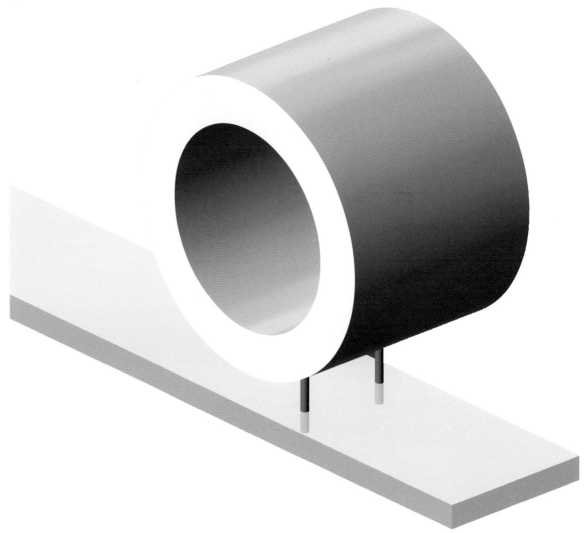

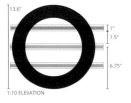

13.6"

1"
1.5"
6.75"

1:10 ELEVATION

LETTER SIZE: HEIGHT 13.5", DEPTH 9"
CLEAR TUBING CONTAINING LED: DIAMETER 1"

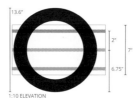

13.6"

2"
7"
6.75"

1:10 ELEVATION

LETTER SIZE: HEIGHT 13.5", DEPTH 9"
CLEAR LEXAN BOX: HEIGHT 7", DEPTH 1"

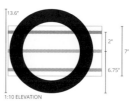

13.6"

2"
7"
6.75"

1:10 ELEVATION

LETTER SIZE: HEIGHT 13.5", DEPTH 9"
CLEAR SHEET: HEIGHT 7", DEPTH 1"
LED LIGHTS AND LETTERS APPLIED

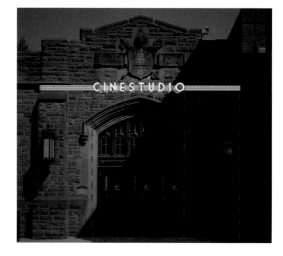

Tata Hall
Harvard Business School
Cambridge, Massachusetts
Interior Wayfinding
and Signage Program

"North" and "South" appear consistently on all the signage elements. The key information is interpreted in large three-dimensional lettering, present at the elevators and other strategic circulation points.

The maintenance department was concerned about having to paint every year around individual letters. To solve the problem, the three-dimensional lettering was grouped onto removable "skewers" that snap into the wall.

Designer
Coco Raynes

Architect
William Rawn Associates

Completed
2013

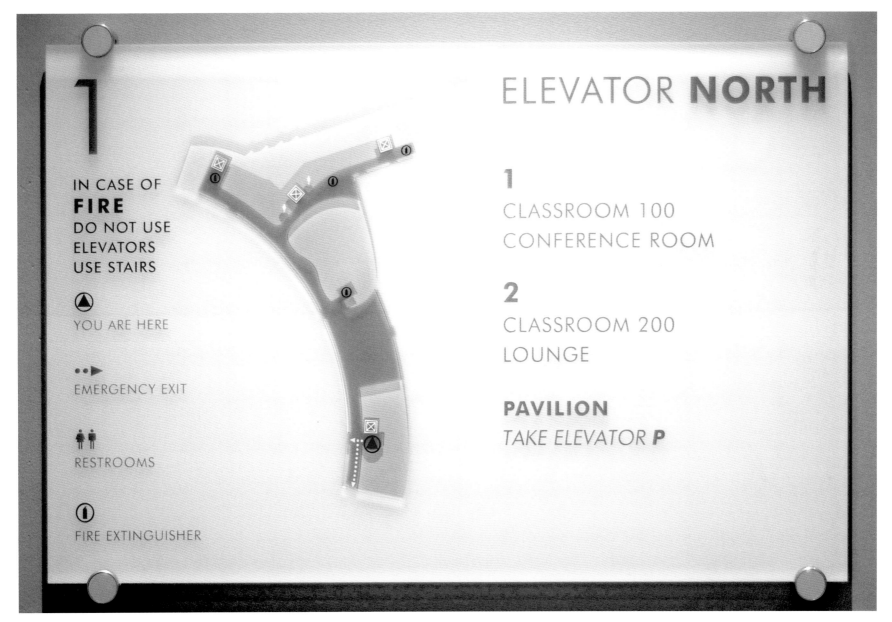

**Grupo Aviatur
Bogotá, Colombia**
Corporate Identity

The Aviatur Group comprises twenty-eight agencies, all related to travel, tourism, or transportation, with branches and offices throughout South America.

Designer
Coco Raynes

Completed
2014

AVIATUR

GRUPO AVIATUR

 UNION **CARGO**

 **AVIA** MARKETING

 **OCTOPUS** TRAVEL

 FUNDACIÓN **AVIATUR**

 **AVIA** CARIBBEAN

 **AVIA** EXPORT

 **AVIATUR** ECOTURISMO

 **AVIA** ISLETA

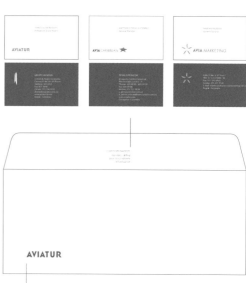

AVIATUR

Above: The typography needed to be simple, strong and bold, easily identified, and adaptable to any scale. Futura was our departure, mixed with our own typographic design.

Above: The old logo, an arrow created in 1962, was no longer valid. However the arrow symbol needed to remain. It became a three-dimensional airplane/arrow, with different color versions and configurations, to better allude to the various agencies products.

Left and below: After studying 100 paper arrows and airplanes, we had finally landed!

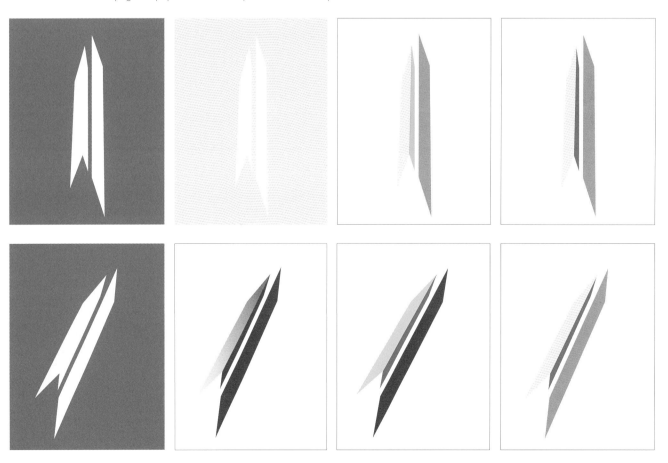

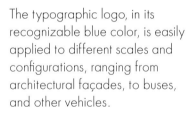

The typographic logo, in its recognizable blue color, is easily applied to different scales and configurations, ranging from architectural façades, to buses, and other vehicles.

The arrow symbol lends itself to elegant fabric patterns for individual matching uniforms of ties and blouses.

The typographic logo permits printing or stamping on any merchandise or object, including coffee cups, folders, and uniforms.

LAS ISLAS...

BARÚ - CARTAGENA DE INDIAS

Las Islas... Hotel, Barú, Colombia
Interior Architecture & Design

The five-star hotel, part of Leading Hotels of the World, belongs to the Group Aviatur. While the logo typography changed, the Aviatur arrow symbol remains, reflecting the colors of the Caribbean Sea.

Architect
Grupo Aviatur

Design consultant
Coco Raynes

Graphic design and signage
Coco Raynes, James France

Completed
2018

Third Award
Global Architecture and Design Award, 2019

This elegant design, based on the principle of extreme simplicity, respects the environment. Only natural Colombian materials, enhanced by superb craftsmanship, were used.

The bungalows are positioned throughout the 32-hectare site, with special attention paid to privacy: guests do not see their neighbors. The habitations along the water's edge have individual pools, while the ones set among the trees have private hot tubs.

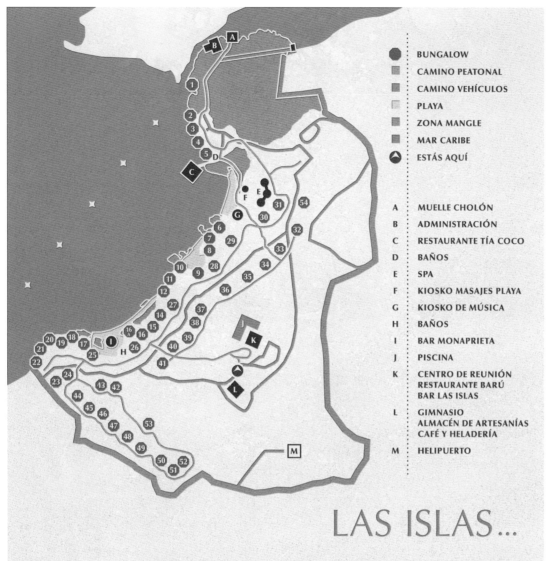

●	BUNGALOW
▢	CAMINO PEATONAL
▢	CAMINO VEHÍCULOS
▢	PLAYA
▢	ZONA MANGLE
▢	MAR CARIBE
◗	ESTÁS AQUÍ

A	MUELLE CHOLÓN
B	ADMINISTRACIÓN
C	RESTAURANTE TÍA COCO
D	BAÑOS
E	SPA
F	KIOSKO MASAJES PLAYA
G	KIOSKO DE MÚSICA
H	BAÑOS
I	BAR MONAPRIETA
J	PISCINA
K	CENTRO DE REUNIÓN RESTAURANTE BARÚ BAR LAS ISLAS
L	GIMNASIO ALMACÉN DE ARTESANÍAS CAFÉ Y HELADERÍA
M	HELIPUERTO

LAS ISLAS...

The signage blends with the wooden fences that delineate the pedestrian and vehicular paths, amid the natural forest and vegetation.

Restoration of a Seventeenth-century Spanish Colonial Residence
Cartagena, Colombia
Design and Interior Architecture

This Spanish Colonial mansion in Colombia's antique city of Cartagena was restored with a modern twist for space and comfort, using the same construction techniques and materials used four centuries ago.

The entire interior space was designed around the remaining four arches and the colonial walls, which were restored.

The architectural finishes were all selected from local materials.

Design and interior architecture
Coco Raynes

Completed
2014

Photography: Fernando Palop (this page and opposite)

Photography: Fernando Palop

Photography: Fernando Palop

Below: The original façade had been altered from its Spanish Colonial appearance to conform to the new Republican architecture, which was retained.

Awards and Recognition

Third Award 2019
Global Architecture and Design Awards, Rethinking the Future

William D. Smith Memorial Award for Preservation and Accessibility 2013
Massachusetts Architectural Access Board

Achievement Award 2013
Boston Preservation Alliance

Silver Award 2012
International Design Award

BSA Design Award 2011
Boston Society of Architects

Women in Design Award of Excellence 2006
Boston Society of Architects

Excellence in Universal Design 2003
Adaptive Environments

Bronze Award CLIO 2003

Bronze Award IDSA 2003
Industrial Designers Society of America

Honor Award SEGD 2002
Society of Environmental Graphic Design

Honor Award USGSA 2002
U.S. General Services Administration

United States Access Board 2001
Design of New Identity, Competition Winner
Society of Environmental Graphic Design

Merit Award SEGD 1998
Society of Environmental Graphic Design

Silver Award IDSA 1997
Industrial Designers Society of America

Bronze Award IDSA 1997
Industrial Designers Society of America

Merit Award SEGD 1997
Society of Environmental Graphic Design

BusinessWeek 1997
Industrial Design Excellence Awards

Merit Award AIAR 1996
American Institute for Architectural Research
Building-Integrated Photovoltaics Design Competition

Gold Award IDSA 1994
Industrial Designers Society of America

Honor Award SEGD 1994
Society of Environmental Graphic Design

Design Distinction Award ID 1994
International Design Magazine

100th Show 1994
American Center for Design

Awards of Excellence
1970, 1977, 1980, 1983, 1985
Art Directors Club of Boston

Award of Excellence for Environmental Graphics
1978
Print Magazine

Award of Excellence 1971
American Institute of Graphic Arts

Competition winner 1967
for Alpha International Corporate Identity
(hotel chain of UTH UnionTouristique Hôtelière)
Paris, France

Publications

BSA Currents January 2020
"Accessibility and Ancient Cities"

BSA Currents March 2017
"Emotion: What the Heart Sees"

BSA Currents January 2016
"On the Tarmac"

Nature Logo October 2015

Architecture Boston October 2014
"The Strange Relationship of Fashion and Architecture"

Architecture and Design vs. Consumerism
August 2012

Novum, Arts December 2009

Axxis December 2008

Boston Globe, Arts December 2006

La Gazette Nord–Pas de Calais December 2005

Architectural Record January 2004

SEGD Design Spring 2003

Aeroports Summer 2002

SEGD / Messages Spring 2002

SEGD / Messages Fall 2001

Boston Globe, Business August 2001

Working With Type, RotoVision SA 2000

This Way Rockport Publishers, 2000

Beautiful Universal Design Wiley & Sons, 2000

El Espectador March 1999

Femina Hebdo February 1999

Evasions January 1999

La Voix Du Mardi January 1999

La Voix Du Nord January 1999

L'hebdo July 1998

El Tiempo Cultura January 1998

Être January 1997

The Japan Times December 1997

Musées March 1997
"Le musée au bout des doigts"

The Boston Herald September 1996

Idéntity July 1996

Plainpied Summer 2006

How Business Annual 1996

Print Art & Design Annual 1995

Novum June 1995

Nikkei Design Japan December 1994

Casa Colombia December 1994

Novum November 1994

Innovation Fall 1994

Interiors August 1994

Architecture August 1994

Boston Globe Arts and Science, August 1994

Interiors August 1994

I.D. Annual Design Review July 1994

Architectural Record July 1994

Progressive Architecture July 1994

BusinessWeek June 1994

Metropolis June 1994

Idéntity March 1994

Health Facilities Management January 1994

SEGD / Messages Winter 1994

The Boston Herald March 1993

International Logos and Trademarks II 1993

Identity Summer 1993

Restaurant Graphics 1992

Hospital Interior Architecture
Van Nostrand Reinhold, 1992

International Logos and Trademarks III 1992

Washington Trademark Design 1992

Sign Design, Van Nostrand Reinhold 1991

Famous Animal Symbols Interecho Press, 1991

SEGD/Messages Newsletter, 1990

American Corporate Identity 4 1989

Environmental Graphic Design USA / East 1989

The Best in Environmental Graphics
Print Casebook 1987, 1988

Architectural Record November 1981

MIT Tech Talk June 1980

Industrial Design July/August 1977

Progressive Architecture February 1977

Hospitals May 1976

Hospitals February 1975

Hospitals (AHAJ) February 1974

Interiors December 1974

Industrial Design November 1974

Interior Design October 1973

Design and Environment Fall 1973

Graphic Annual Packaging 1970

Thank you to all my collaborators for their dedication, talent, and patience through this long journey, especially to James France, without whom this book would not have come through. To my clients for their trust and friendship, and to my life-long manufacturers, especially MS Signs, Inc., who supported my visions and accepted to do things differently.

And to my extraordinary children, Samantha and Ben, for understanding that the design profession is a vocation beyond nine to five.

— Coco Raynes

Published in Australia in 2020 by
The Images Publishing Group Pty Ltd
ABN 89 059 734 431

Offices

Melbourne
6 Bastow Place
Mulgrave, Victoria 3170
Australia
Tel: +61 3 9561 5544

New York
6 West 18th Street 4B
New York City, NY 10011
United States
Tel: +1 212 645 1111

Shanghai
6F, Building C, 838 Guangji Road
Hongkou District, Shanghai 200434
China
Tel: +86 021 31260822

books@imagespublishing.com
www.imagespublishing.com

Copyright © Coco Raynes 2020
The Images Publishing Group Reference Number: 1582

A catalogue record for this
book is available from the
National Library of Australia

Title: Coco Raynes: 50 Years of Design Evolution // Coco Raynes Associates, Inc.
ISBN: 9781864708899

Book design by Coco Raynes and James France

This title was commissioned in IMAGES' Melbourne office and produced as follows:
Editorial Georgia (Gina) Tsarouhas, *Graphic design* Ryan Marshall,
Art direction/production Nicole Boehringer

Printed on 150gsm Magno Matt art paper at Graphius nv, in Belgium